A Gentle Thunder

Max Lucado

A Gentle Thunder

Hearing God Through the Storm

W PUBLISHING GROUP™

www.wpublishinggroup.com

A Division of Thomas Nelson, Inc.
www.ThomasNelson.com

Published by W Publishing Group, a Division of Thomas Nelson, Inc., P.O. Box 141000, Nashville, Tennessee, 37214.

Unless otherwise indicated, Scripture quotations used in this book are from the Holy Bible, New Century Version, copyright © 1987, 1988, 1991 by W Publishing Group, a Division of Thomas Nelson, Inc., P.O. Box 141000, Nashville, Tennessee 37214. Used by permission.

Other references are from the following sources: The Holy Bible, New International Version (NIV). Copyright © 1973, 1978, 1984 International Bible Society. Used by permission of Zondervan Bible Publishers. *The Living Bible* (TLB), copyright 1971 by Tyndale House Publishers, Wheaton, Ill. Used by permission. The New English Bible (NEB). Copyright © 1961, 1970 by the Delegates of the Oxford University Press and the Syndics of the Cambridge University Press. Reprinted by permission. *The Message* (TM), copyright © 1993. Used by permission of NavPress Publishing Group.

Anecdotes in this volume are based on fact; however in some instances details have been changed to protect identities.

Book Design by Mark McGarry
Set in Janson

LIBRARY OF CONGRESS CATALOGING-IN-PUBLICATION DATA
Lucado, Max
A Gentle Thunder / Max Lucado.
p. cm.
ISBN 0-8499-1138-9 (HARDCOVER)
ISBN 0-8499-4324-8 (TP)
(INCLUDES BIBLIOGRAPHICAL REFERENCES).
1. Bible. N.T. John—Meditations. 2. Consolation. 3. Christian life. I. Title.

BS2615.4.L83 1995
242'.5–dc20
95-19816
CIP

02 03 05 05 PHX 5 4
Printed in the United States of America.

In honor of the past,
in anticipation of the future,
I dedicate this book to
Kip Jordon and Byron Williamson
of W Publishing Group.

A Gentle Thunder

And the Angels Were Silent

The Applause of Heaven

God Came Near

The Great House of God

He Chose the Nails

He Still Moves Stones

In the Eye of the Storm

In the Grip of Grace

Just in Case You Ever Wonder

Just Like Jesus

No Wonder They Call Him the Savior

On the Anvil

Six Hours One Friday

Tell Me the Secrets

Tell Me the Story

Traveling Light

When Christ Comes

When God Whispers Your Name

Contents

Contents

OUR CHOICE

Contents

Acknowledgments

A BOOK should be a garden that fits in the hands. Word-petals of color. Stems of strength. Roots of truth. Turn a page and turn the seasons. Read the sentence and enjoy the roses.

No gardening is easy, however, especially that of words. Weeds sprout and ideas wilt. Some paragraphs need water; others need the shears. There are times when you wonder if this jungle can ever be trimmed. I am deeply grateful to some folks who rolled up their sleeves, got down in the soil, and joined me in the work.

Karen Hill: my assistant and dear friend. Loyal, creative, and always willing to help. You are invaluable.

Liz Heaney: my longtime editor. Though I wince when you prune, no shears are truer.

Steve Halliday: Another great job with the discussion guide.

The staff and members of the Oak Hills Church: What a field of faith!

The '94 edition of the Young Messiah Tour: Thanks for listening to these words before they were weeded.

W Publishing Group: No team does better!

Lynn Anderson: My first purchase after leaving college was a set of your sermons on the Gospel of John. Because you loved John then, I love him today.

Steve and Cheryl Green: For doing all that you do so I could do this.

Lindsey Hill, Lois Jeane Davis, Jeanette Rudd, Becky Bryant, Tina Chisholm, and Francis Rose, the staff of UpWords Radio Ministry: angels on loan.

Sue Ann Jones: What a sharp eye and skillful pen!

Jenna, Andrea, and Sara: May you always be rooted in the soil of his love.

And for Denalyn, my wife: For making the grass so green on this side of the fence that the other side looks barren.

And finally, for you, the reader: Of the many gardens you could visit, you've chosen to visit this one. I'm honored. I hope your stay is delightful. May you find familiar things new, and new things familiar.

Stay as long as you like. If you find a rose worth keeping, feel free to clip it. If you find a few worth sharing, please do.

And who knows? Adam heard God speak in a garden; maybe the same will happen to you.

When you were in trouble, you called,
and I saved you.
I answered you with thunder.

Psalm 81:7

His Voice, Our Choice

A GOOD PILOT does what it takes to get his passengers home.

I saw a good example of this while flying somewhere over Missouri. The flight attendant told us to take our seats because of impending turbulence. It was a rowdy flight, and the folks weren't quick to respond; so she warned us again. "The flight is about to get bumpy. For your own safety, take your seats."

Most did. But a few didn't, so she changed her tone, "Ladies and gentlemen, for your own good, take your seats."

I thought everyone was seated. But apparently I was wrong, for the next voice we heard was that of the pilot. "This is Captain Brown," he advised. "People have gotten hurt by going to the bathroom instead of staying in their seats. Let's be very clear about our responsibilities. My job is to get you through the storm. Your job is to do what I say. Now sit down and buckle up!"

About that time the bathroom door opened, and a red-faced fellow with a sheepish grin exited and took his seat.

Was the pilot wrong in what he did? Was the pilot being insensitive or unthoughtful? No, just the opposite. He would rather the man be safe and embarrassed than uninformed and hurt.

Good pilots do what it takes to get their passengers home.

So does God. Here is a key question. How far do you want God to go in getting your attention? If God has to choose between your eternal safety and your earthly comfort, which do you hope he chooses? Don't answer too quickly. Give it some thought.

If God sees you standing when you should be sitting, if God sees you at risk rather than safe, how far do you want him to go in getting your attention?

What if he moved you to another land? (As he did Abraham.) What if he called you out of retirement? (Remember Moses?) How about the voice of an angel or the bowel of a fish? (À la Gideon and Jonah.) How about a promotion like Daniel's or a demotion like Samson's?

God does what it takes to get our attention. Isn't that the message of the Bible? Isn't that *the* message of the Bible? The relentless pursuit of God. God on the hunt. God in the search. Peeking under the bed for hiding kids, stirring the bushes for lost sheep. Cupping hand to mouth and shouting into the canyon. Wrestling with us Jacobs in the muddy Jabboks of life.

For all its peculiarities and unevenness, the Bible has a simple story. God made man. Man rejected God. God won't give up until he wins him back. From Moses in Moab to John on Patmos, the voice can be heard: "I'm the pilot. You're the passenger. My job is to get you home. Your job is to do what I say."

God is as creative as he is relentless. The same hand that sent manna to Israel sent Uzzah to his death. The same hand that set the children free from Israel also sent them captive to Babylon. Both kind and stern. Tender and tough. Faithfully firm. Patiently urgent. Eagerly tolerant. Softly shouting. Gently thundering.

Gentle thunder.

That's how John saw Jesus. John's Gospel has two themes: the voice of God and the choice of man. And since this book is based on John, you'll see the same tandem: His voice. Our choice.

Jesus said, "I am the bread that gives life. I am the light of the world. I am the resurrection and the life. I am the light of the world. I am the door. I am the way, the truth, and the life. I will come back and take you with me."

Jesus proclaiming—ever offering but never forcing:

> Standing over the crippled man: "Do you want to be well?" (John 5:6).

> Eye to eye with the blind man, now healed: "Do you believe in the Son of Man?" (John 9:35).

> Near the tomb of Lazarus, probing the heart of Martha: "Everyone who lives and believes in me will never die. Martha, do you believe this?" (John 11:26).

> Testing Pilate's motive: "Is that your own question, or did others tell you about me?" (John 18:34).

The first time John hears Jesus speak, Jesus asks a question, "What are you looking for?" (John 1:38). Among Jesus' last words is yet another: "Do you love me?" (21:17).

This is the Jesus John remembers. The honest questions. The thundering claims. The gentle touch. Never going where not invited, but once invited never stopping until he's finished, until a choice has been made.

God will whisper. He will shout. He will touch and tug. He will take away our burdens; he'll even take away our blessings. If there are a thousand steps between us and him, he will take all but one. But he will leave the final one for us. The choice is ours.

Please understand. His goal is not to make you happy. His goal is to make you his. His goal is not to get you what you want; it is to get you what you need. And if that means a jolt or two to get you in your seat, then be jolted. Earthly discomfort is a glad swap for heavenly peace. Jesus said, "In this world you will have trouble, but be brave! I have defeated the world" (John 16:33).

How could he speak with such authority? What gave him the right to take command? Simple. He, like the pilot, knows what we don't, and he can see what we can't.

What did the pilot know? He knew how to fly the plane.

What did the pilot see? Storm clouds ahead.

What does God know? He knows how to navigate history.

What does God see? I think you get the message.

God wants to get you home safely.

Just think of him as your pilot. Think of yourself as his passenger. Consider this book as in-flight reading—and think twice before you get up to go to the potty.

His Voice

Once there was a man who dared God to speak.

Burn the bush like you did for Moses, God.
  And I will follow.

Collapse the walls like you did for Joshua, God.
  And I will fight.

Still the waves like you did on Galilee, God.
  And I will listen.

And so the man sat by a bush, near a wall, close to the sea
  and waited for God to speak.

And God heard the man, so God answered.
He sent fire, not for a bush, but for a church.
    He brought down a wall, not of brick, but of sin.
        He stilled a storm, not of the sea, but of a soul.

And God waited for the man to respond.
And he waited . . .
        And he waited . . .
            And waited.

But because the man was looking at bushes, not hearts;
    bricks and not lives, seas and not souls,
        he decided that God had done nothing.
Finally he looked to God and asked, *Have you lost your power?*
And God looked at him and said, *Have you lost your hearing?*

In the beginning was the Word. . . .
The Word became a human and lived among us.

John 1:1, 14

The Author of Life
The God Who Dreamed

SEATED AT THE great desk, the Author opens the large book. It has no words. It has no words because no words exist. No words exist because no words are needed. There are no ears to hear them, no eyes to read them. The Author is alone.

And so he takes the great pen and begins to write. Like an artist gathers his colors and a woodcarver his tools, the Author assembles his words.

There are three. Three single words. Out of these three will pour a million thoughts. But on these three words, the story will suspend.

He takes his quill and spells the first. *T-i-m-e*.

Time did not exist until he wrote it. He, himself, is timeless, but his story would be encased in time. The story would have a first rising of the sun, a first shifting of the sand. A beginning . . . and an end. A final chapter. He knows it before he writes it.

Time. A footspan on eternity's trail.

Slowly, tenderly, the Author writes the second word. A name. *A-d-a-m*.

As he writes, he sees him, the first Adam. Then he sees all the others. In a thousand eras in a thousand lands, the Author sees them. Each Adam. Each child. Instantly loved. Permanently loved. To each he assigns a time. To each he appoints a place. No accidents. No coincidences. Just design.

The Author makes a promise to these unborn: *In my image, I will make you. You will be like me. You will laugh. You will create. You will never die. And you will write.*

They must. For each life is a book, not to be read, but rather a story to be written. The Author starts each life story, but each life will write his or her own ending.

What a dangerous liberty. How much safer it would have been to finish the story for each Adam. To script every option. It would have been simpler. It would have been safer. But it would not have been love. Love is only love if chosen.

So the Author decides to give each child a pen. "Write carefully," he whispers.

Lovingly, deliberately, he writes the third word, already feeling the pain. *E-m-m-a-n-u-e-l.*

The greatest mind in the universe imagined time. The truest judge granted Adam a choice. But it was love that gave Emmanuel, God with us.

The Author would enter his own story.

The Word would become flesh. He, too, would be born. He, too, would be human. He, too, would have feet and hands. He, too, would have tears and trials.

And most importantly, he, too, would have a choice. Emmanuel would stand at the crossroads of life and death and make a choice.

The Author knows well the weight of that decision. He pauses as he writes the page of his own pain. He could stop. Even the Author has a choice. But how can a Creator not create? How can a Writer not write? And how can Love not love? So he chooses life, though it means death, with hope that his children will do the same.

And so the Author of Life completes the story. He drives the spike in the flesh and rolls the stone over the grave. Knowing the choice he will make, knowing the choice all Adams will make, he pens, "The End," then closes the book and proclaims the beginning.

"Let there be light!"

I saw the Spirit come down in the form of a dove and rest on him. Until then I did not know who the Christ was. But the God who sent me to baptize with water told me, "You will see the Spirit come down and rest on a man; he is the One who will baptize with the Holy Spirit." I have seen this happen, and I tell you the truth: This is the Son of God.

John 1:32–34

The Hound of Heaven
The God Who Pursues

JOHN THE BAPTIST saw a dove and believed. James Whittaker saw a sea gull and believed. Who's to say the one who sent the first didn't send the second?

James Whittaker was a member of the handpicked crew that flew the B-17 Flying Fortress captained by Eddie Rickenbacker. Anybody who remembers October of 1942 remembers the day Rickenbacker and his crew were reported lost at sea.

Somewhere over the Pacific, out of radio range, the plane ran out of fuel and crashed into the ocean. The nine men spent the next month floating in three rafts. They battled the heat, the storms, and the water. Sharks, some ten feet long, would ram their nine-foot boats. After only eight days their rations were eaten or destroyed by saltwater. It would take a miracle to survive.

One morning after their daily devotions, Rickenbacker leaned his head back against the raft and pulled his hat over his eyes. A bird landed on his head. He peered out from under his hat. Every eye was on him. He instinctively knew it was a sea gull.

Rickenbacker caught it, and the crew ate it. The bird's intestines were used for bait to catch fish . . . and the crew survived to tell the story. A story about a stranded crew with no hope or help in sight.

A story about prayers offered and prayers answered. A story about a visitor from an unknown land traveling a great distance to give his life as a sacrifice.

A story of salvation.

A story much like our own. Weren't we, like the crew, stranded? Weren't we, like the crew, praying? And weren't we, like the crew, rescued by a visitor we've never seen through a sacrifice we'll never forget?

You may have heard the Rickenbacker story before. You may have even heard it from me. You may have read it in one of my books. Coreen Schwenk did. She was engaged to the only crew member who did not survive, young Sgt. Alex Kacymarcyck. As a result of a 1985 reunion of the crew, Mrs. Schwenk learned that the widow of James Whittaker lived only eighty miles from her house. The two women met and shared their stories.

After reading this story in my book *In the Eye of the Storm*, Mrs. Schwenk felt compelled to write to me. The real miracle, she informed me, was not a bird on the head of Eddie Rickenbacker but a change in the heart of James Whittaker. The greatest event of that day was not the rescue of a crew but the rescue of a soul.

James Whittaker was an unbeliever. The plane crash didn't change his unbelief. The days facing death didn't cause him to reconsider his destiny. In fact, Mrs. Whittaker said her husband grew irritated with John Bartak, a crew member who continually read his Bible privately and aloud.

But his protests didn't stop Bartak from reading. Nor did Whittaker's resistance stop the Word from penetrating his soul. Unknown to Whittaker, the soil of his heart was being plowed. For it was one morning after a Bible reading that the sea gull landed on Captain Rickenbacker's head.

And at that moment Jim became a believer.

I chuckled when I read the letter. Not at the letter; I believe every word of it. Nor at James Whittaker. I have every reason to believe his conversion was real. But I had to chuckle at . . . please excuse me . . . I had to chuckle at God.

Isn't that just like him? Who would go to such extremes to save a soul? Such an effort to get a guy's attention. The rest of the world is occupied with Germany and Hitler. Every headline is reporting the actions of Roosevelt and Churchill. The globe is locked in a battle for freedom . . . and the Father is in the Pacific sending a missionary pigeon to save a soul. Oh, the lengths to which God will go to get our attention and win our affection.

In 1893 Francis Thompson, a Roman Catholic poet, described God as the "Hound of Heaven":

> I fled Him, down the nights and down the days;
> I fled Him, down the arches of the years;
> I fled Him, down the labyrinthian ways
> > Of my own mind; and in the mist of tears
> I hid from Him, and under running laughter,
> > Up vestaed hopes I sped
> And shot precipitated
> Adown Titanic glooms.[1]

Thompson speaks of Jesus as "that tremendous lover, pursuing me with his love." Jesus follows with "unhurrying chase and unperturbed pace, deliberate speed, majestic instancy." And in the end Jesus speaks, reminding us, "Alas, thou knowest not how little worthy of any love thou art. Whom wilt thou find to love ignoble thee, save me, save only me? For that which I took from thee I did but take, not for thy harm but that thou might seek it in my arms."[2]

Do you have room for such a picture of God? Can you see God as the "tremendous lover, pursuing us with his love"? During the first week of Jesus' ministry he calls his first disciples. Why do they come? Who influences their choice? Note the verbs associated with Jesus in John 1.

Jesus turned . . . v. 38
Jesus asked . . . v. 38
Jesus answered . . . v. 39
Jesus looked . . . v. 42

Jesus decided . . . v. 43

Jesus found . . . v. 43

It's clear who does the work. If anyone is in Christ, it is because Christ has called him or her. Christ may use a sermon. He may inspire a conversation. He may speak through a song. But in every case Christ is the One who calls.

Consider these examples:

One evening, John Wesley entered a brief account in his journal. He wrote of going unwillingly to a meeting of a society in Aldersgate Street in London where one of the group was reading the preface to Luther's *Commentary on the Epistle to the Romans*. Did you get the picture? He went unwillingly, a stranger to a small group, listening to a two-hundred-year-old piece of literature. And yet he wrote, "About a quarter before nine I felt my heart strangely warmed."[3]

In his classic work *Confessions*, Augustine tells of the turning point in his life. Torn between the temptation of a mistress and the quiet call of the Spirit of God, he was sitting on a bench under a fig tree, his Bible open, his eyesight fogged by tears. He heard a voice calling from a neighboring house, "Pick it up . . . Pick it up . . ."

The voice was not addressed to Augustine; no doubt children were calling to one another in a game. However, the voice stirred Augustine in his solitude, and he did what the voice commanded. He picked up his Bible and read it. The passage before him was Romans 13:13–14: "Let us live in a right way, like people who belong to the day. We should not have wild parties or get drunk. There should be no sexual sins of any kind, no fighting or jealousy. But clothe yourselves with the Lord Jesus Christ and forget about satisfying your sinful self."

He heard the voice of God, bade farewell to his mistress, and followed Christ.[4]

Novelist Frederick Buechner was twenty-seven years old and living alone in New York City, trying to write a book when he, a non-churchgoer, went to church. On impulse. The preacher spoke on the topic of crowning Christ in your heart. Jesus refused the crown of Satan in the wilderness but accepts the crown of his people when we confess him. The preacher went on for quite some time with words that sounded nice but didn't stick.

But then he said something that Buechner never forgot. I'll let him tell you:

> And then with his head bobbing up and down so that his glasses tittered, he said in his odd sandy voice, the voice of an old nurse, that the coronation of Jesus took place among confession and tears and, as God is my witness, great laughter, he said. Jesus is crowned among confession and tears and great laughter, and at that phrase great laughter, for reasons I have never satisfactorily understood, the great wall of China crumbled and Atlantis rose up out of the sea, and on Madison Avenue, at 73rd Street, tears leapt from my eyes as though I had been struck in the face.[5]

Too bizarre? Think for a moment about your world. Remember that voice, that face, that event? Wasn't there a time when the common bush of the wilderness was ablaze with a voice that left you stuttering? For Wesley it was a reading, for Augustine the voice of a child, and for Buechner a call to laughter.

And for you? The extended hand of a bag woman? The birth of your child? The tears of the widower? The explosion of a sunset? The impassioned sermon that moved all? The dull sermon that moved none—but you?

It isn't the circumstance that matters; it is God in the circumstance. It isn't the words; it is God speaking them. It wasn't the mud that healed the eyes of the blind man; it was the finger of God in the mud. The cradle and the cross were as common as grass. What made them holy was the One laid upon them. The dove and the gull weren't special. But the One who sent them was.

Amazing, the lengths to which God will go to get our attention.

Nathanael said to Philip, "Can anything good come from Nazareth?"
Philip answered, "Come and see."

John 1:46

Come and See

The God Who Came

THE FIRST ANSWER given the first doubter is the only one necessary.

When Nathanael doubted that anything good could come out of Nazareth, Philip's response was simply, "Come and see."

Nathanael's question remains: "Can anything good come out of Nazareth?" Have two thousand years of Christianity changed this world? Is the life of the young Nazarene carpenter really worth considering?

The question still lingers.

And the answer of Philip still suffices. Come and see.

Come and see the rock that has withstood the winds of time. Hear his voice.

> The truth undaunted,
> > grace unspotted,
> > > loyalty undeterred.

Come and see the flame that tyrants and despots have not extinguished.

Come and see the passion that oppression has not squelched.

Come and see the hospitals and orphanages rising beside the crumbling ruins of humanism and atheism. Come and see what Christ has done.

Come and see the great drama threading through twenty centuries of history and art.

> Handel weeping as he composes *The Messiah*.
>
> Da Vinci sighing as he portrays the Last Supper.
>
> Michelangelo stepping back from the rock-carved David and bidding the stone to speak.

Can anything good come out of Nazareth? Come and see.

> See Wilberforce fighting to free slaves in England— because he believed.
>
> See Washington at prayer in Valley Forge—because he believed.
>
> See Lincoln alone with a dog-eared Bible—because he believed.

Can anything good come out of Nazareth? Come and see.
Come and see the changed lives:
    the alcoholic now dry,
        the embittered now joyful,
            the shamed now forgiven.
Come and see the marriages rebuilt, the orphans embraced, the imprisoned inspired.
Journey into the jungles and hear the drums beating in praise.
Sneak into the corners of communism and find believers worshiping under threat of death.
Walk on death row and witness the prisoner condemned by man yet liberated by God.
Venture into the gulags and dungeons of the world and hear the songs of the saved refusing to be silent.
Can anything good come out of Nazareth?

Come and see the pierced hand of God touch the most common heart, wipe the tear from the wrinkled face, and forgive the ugliest sin.

Come and see.

Come and see the tomb. The tomb once occupied, now vacant; the grave once sealed, now empty. Cynics have raised their theories, doubters have raised their questions. But their musings continue to melt in the bright light of Easter morning.

Come and see. He avoids no seeker. He ignores no probe. He fears no search. Come and see. Nathanael came. And Nathanael saw. And Nathanael discovered, "Teacher, you are the Son of God; you are the King of Israel."

It was dark now, and Jesus had not yet come to them.

John 6:17

Miracle at Midnight

The God of Perfect Timing

L ET ME SHARE with you the thoughts of a young missionary. What follows are phrases excerpted from his journal during his first month on the mission field.

On the flight to the field he writes: "The next time this plane touches down, I will be a missionary. For good! Yes, finally. To God be the glory."

The second day he reflects: "I keep reminding myself that the homesickness is temporary—it comes with the weariness and adjustments. That doesn't remove it, though. I must remember the reason I'm here. Not for my own joy or gain, but for the growth of God's kingdom."

By day number three his spirits are up: "God, it's a grand blessing to serve you. The people are so friendly . . . the mountains are so pretty . . . our friends are so gracious."

But on the fourth day his spirits sag: "It's difficult for us to think about home. We cried this morning."

On the fifth day he doesn't rebound: "Today is not so clear. The clouds have buried the mountains. The sky is gray."

By day six, the storm is coming in: "Yesterday was the toughest day thus far. The newness is gone. I'm tired of this language. We were blue all day. We could hardly think of our family and friends without weeping."

On the eighth day the waves have crested, and the winds are blowing: "This hotel room which has been our home is cold and impersonal. The tall ceiling, the strange walls . . . the unfamiliar surroundings. I held my wife as she wept, and we both confessed the ugliness of the thought of spending the rest of our lives in this foreign country. It's hard. We're so far from home."

By the tenth day the gales are at full force: "Doggone it, I know God is guiding us, I know he has a plan for us, but it's so hard. When will we find a house? How will we learn this language? Lord, forgive my sorry attitude."

And just when you'd think it couldn't get any darker: "I wish I could say I'm thrilled to be here. I'm not. I'm only willing to be here. This last week was as tough as I've ever had anywhere. My commitment to be a missionary feels like a prison sentence."

I know well the frustration behind those words—I wrote them. I remember my confusion. Hadn't Denalyn and I obeyed God? Didn't God send us to Brazil? Wasn't this his plan? Weren't we just doing what we were told?

Doesn't peace always follow obedience? (Why are you smiling?)

Perhaps the disciples had the same expectation. They only did what they were told. Jesus told them to get into the boat, so they did. They didn't question the order; they simply obeyed it. They could have objected. After all, it was evening and darkness was only minutes away. But Jesus told them to get into the boat, so they did.

What was the result of their obedience? John's crisp description will tell you: "That evening Jesus' followers went down to

Lake Galilee. It was dark, and Jesus had not yet come to them. The followers got into a boat and started across the lake to Capernaum. By now a strong wind was blowing, and the waves on the lake were getting bigger" (John 6:16–17).

What a chilling phrase, "Jesus had not yet come to them." Caught in the storm of the "not yet." They did exactly what Jesus said, and look what it got them! A night on a storm-tossed sea with their Master somewhere on the shore.

It's one thing to suffer for doing wrong. Something else entirely to suffer for doing right. But it happens. And when the storm bursts, it washes away the naive assumption that if I do right, I will never suffer.

Just ask the faithful couple whose crib is empty and whose womb is barren.

Just ask the businessman whose honest work was rewarded with runaway inflation.

Just ask the student who took a stand for the truth and got mocked, the Sunday school teacher who took a class and got tired, the husband who took a chance and forgave his wife, only to be betrayed again.

And so the winds blow.

And so the boat bounces.

And so the disciples wonder, "Why the storm, and where is Jesus?" It's bad enough to be in the storm, but to be in the storm alone?

The disciples had been on the sea for about nine hours.[1] John tells us they rowed four miles (John 6:19). That's a long night. How many times did they search the darkness for their Master? How many times did they call out his name?

Why did he take so long?

Why does he take so long?

I think I hear the answer in the next room. As I write, I can hear my ten-year-old daughter playing the piano. She has just begun her second year. Her teacher recently upped the ante. No more rinky-dink songs; no more nursery rhymes. It's time to move on. Now the rhythm varies, the notes sharpen, and the key changes. It will be pleasant to the ear . . . someday.

But today the notes come slowly and the fingers drag and Jenna would quit if given the chance. Am I a cruel father for urging her to continue? Am I unfair in prodding her to practice? I'm not oblivious to her struggle. I can hear it. I'm not blind to her tears. I can see them. I know she'd be much happier swimming or reading or watching television.

Then why do I let her suffer?

Because I love her. And I know that a struggle today will result in music tomorrow.

Mark tells us that during the storm Jesus "saw his followers struggling" (Mark 6:48). Through the night he saw them. Through the storm he saw them. And like a loving father he waited. He waited until the right time, until the right moment. He waited until he knew it was time to come, and then he came.

What made it the right time? I don't know. Why was the ninth hour better than the fourth or fifth? I can't answer that. Why does God wait until the money is gone? Why does he wait until the sickness has lingered? Why does he choose to wait until the other side of the grave to answer the prayers for healing?

I don't know. I only know his timing is always right. I can only say he will do what is best. "God will always give what is right to his people who cry to him night and day, and he will not be slow to answer them" (Luke 18:7).

Though you hear nothing, he is speaking. Though you see nothing, he is acting. With God there are no accidents. Every incident is intended to bring us closer to him.

Can I give a great example? The direct route from Egypt to Israel would take only eleven days by foot.[2] But God took the Israelites on the long road, which took forty years. Why did he do that? Read carefully the explanation.

Remember how the LORD your God has led you in the desert for these forty years, taking away your pride and testing you, because he wanted to know what was in your heart. He took away your pride when he let you get hungry, and then he fed you with manna, which neither you nor your ancestors had ever seen. This was to teach you that a person does not live by eating only bread, but by everything the LORD says. During these forty years, your clothes did not wear out, and your feet did not swell. Know in your heart that the LORD your God corrects you as a parent corrects a child. (Deut. 8:2–4)

Look what God did in the desert. He took away the Israelites' pride. He tested their hearts. He proved that he would provide for them. Did God want the children of Israel to reach the Promised Land? Of course. But he was more concerned that they arrive prepared than that they arrive soon.

It reminds me of the often-told story of two maestros who attended a concert to hear a promising young soprano. One commented on the purity of her voice. The other responded, "Yes, but she'll sing better once her heart is broken." There are certain passions only learned by pain. And there are times when God, knowing that, allows us to endure the pain for the sake of the song.

So what does God do while we are enduring the pain? What does he do while we are in the storm? You'll love this. He prays for us. Jesus wasn't in the boat because he had gone to the hills to pray (see Mark 6:46). Jesus prayed. That is remarkable. It is even more remarkable that Jesus didn't stop praying when his disciples were struggling. When he heard their cries, he remained in prayer.

Why? Two possible answers. Either he didn't care, or he believed in prayer. I think you know the correct choice.

And you know what? Jesus hasn't changed. He still prays for his disciples. "Because Jesus lives forever, he will never stop serving as priest. So he is able always to save those who come to God through him because he always lives, asking God to help them" (Heb. 7:24–25).

So where does that leave us? While Jesus is praying and we are in the storm, what are we to do? Simple. We do what the disciples did. We row. The disciples rowed most of the night. Mark says they "struggled hard" to row the boat (Mark 6:48). The word *struggle* is elsewhere translated as "tormented." Wasn't easy. Wasn't glamorous.

Much of life is spent rowing. Getting out of bed. Fixing lunches. Turning in assignments. Changing diapers. Paying bills. Routine. Regular. More struggle than strut. More wrestling than resting.

When Denalyn and I went to Brazil, we thought the life of a missionary was one of daily charm and fascination. A Christian Indiana Jones. We learned otherwise.

You have, too? You thought marriage was going to be a lifelong date? You thought having kids was going to be like baby-sitting? You thought the company who hired you wanted to hear all the ideas you had in college?

Then you learned otherwise. The honeymoon ended. The IRS called, and the boss wanted you to spend the week in Muleshoe, Texas. Much of life is spent rowing.

Oh, there are moments of glamour, days of celebration. We have our share of feasts, but we also have our share of baloney sandwiches. And to have the first we must endure the second.

As things turned out, Denalyn and I had five wonderful years in Brazil. And we learned that at the right time, God comes. In the right way, he appears. So don't bail out. Don't give up! Don't lay down the oars! He is too wise to forget you, too loving to hurt you. When you can't see him, trust him. He is praying a prayer that he himself will answer.

Jesus knew that the father had given him power over everything and that he had come from God and was going back to God. So during the meal Jesus stood up and took off his outer clothing. Taking a towel, he wrapped it around his waist. Then he poured water into a bowl and began to wash the followers' feet, drying them with the towel that was wrapped around him.

John 13:3–5

5

The Secret of Forgiveness
The God of Great Grace

IT'S NOT EASY watching Jesus wash these feet.

To see the hands of God massaging the toes of men is, well . . . it's not right. The disciples should be washing his feet. Nathanael should pour the water. Andrew should carry the towel. But they don't. No one does. Rather than serve, they argue over which one is the greatest (Luke 22:24).

What disappointment their words must have brought Jesus.

"I'm the number one apostle."

"No, I'm much more spiritual than you."

"You guys are crazy. I brought more people to hear Jesus than anyone."

As they argue, the basin sits in the corner, untouched. The towel lies on the floor, unused. The servant's clothing hangs on the wall, unworn. Each disciple sees these things. Each disciple knows their purpose. But no one moves, except Jesus. As they bicker, he stands.

But he doesn't speak. He removes his robe and takes the servant's wrap off of the wall. Taking the pitcher, he pours the water into the basin. He kneels before them with the basin and sponge and begins

33

to wash. The towel that covers his waist is also the towel that dries their feet.

It's not right.

Isn't it enough that these hands will be pierced in the morning? Must they scrub grime tonight? And the disciples . . . do they deserve to have their feet washed? Their affections have waned; their loyalties have wavered.

We want to say . . .

Look at John, Jesus. This is the same John who told you to destroy a city. The same John who demanded that you censure a Christ-follower who wasn't in your group. Why are you washing his feet?

And James! Skip James. He wanted the seat of honor. He and his brother wanted special treatment. Don't give it to him. Give him the towel. Let him wash his own feet. Let him learn a lesson.

And while you are at it, Jesus, you might as well skip Philip. He told you there wasn't enough food to feed the large crowd. You tested him, and he flunked. You gave him the chance, and he blew it.

And Peter? Sure, these are the feet that walked on water, but they're also the feet that thrashed about in the deep. He didn't believe you. Sure he confessed you as the Christ, but he's also the one who told you that you didn't have to die. He doesn't deserve to have his feet washed.

None of them do. When you were about to be stoned in Nazareth, did they come to your defense? When the Pharisees took up rocks to kill you, did they volunteer to take your place? You know what they have done.

And what's more, you know what they are about to do!

You can already hear them snoring in the garden. They say they'll stay awake, but they won't. You'll sweat blood; they'll saw logs.

You can hear them sneaking away from the soldiers. They make promises tonight. They'll make tracks tomorrow.

Look around the table, Jesus. Out of the twelve, how many will stand with you in Pilate's court? How many will share with you the Roman whip? And when you fall under the weight of the cross, which disciple will be close enough to spring to your side and carry your burden?

None of them will. Not one. A stranger will be called because no disciple will be near.

Don't wash their feet, Jesus. Tell them to wash yours.

That's what we want to say. Why? Because of the injustice? Because we don't want to see our King behaving as a servant? God on his hands and knees, his hair hanging around his face? Do we object because we don't want to see God washing feet?

Or do we object because we don't want to do the same?

Stop and think for a minute. Don't we have some people like the disciples in our world?

Double-tongued promise-breakers. Fair-weather friends. What they said and what they did are two different things. Oh, maybe they didn't leave you alone at the cross, but maybe they left you alone with the bills . . .

   or your question

                 or your illness.

Or maybe you were just left at the altar,

                 or in the cold,

                           holding the bag.

Vows forgotten. Contract abandoned.

Logic says: "Put up your fists."

Jesus says: "Fill up the basin."

Logic says: "Bloody his nose."

Jesus says: "Wash his feet."

Logic says: "She doesn't deserve it."

Jesus says: "You're right, but you don't, either."

I don't understand how God can be so kind to us, but he is. He kneels before us, takes our feet in his hands, and washes them. Please understand that in washing the disciples' feet, Jesus is washing ours. You and I are in this story. We are at the table. That's us being cleansed, not from our dirt, but from our sins.

And the cleansing is not just a gesture; it is a necessity. Listen to what Jesus said: "If I don't wash your feet, you are not one of my people" (John 13:8).

Jesus did not say, "If you don't wash your feet." Why not? Because we cannot. We cannot cleanse our own filth. We cannot remove our own sin. Our feet must be in his hands.

Don't miss the meaning here. To place our feet in the basin of Jesus is to place the filthiest parts of our lives into his hands. In the ancient East, people's feet were caked with mud and dirt. The servant of the feast saw to it that the feet were cleaned. Jesus is assuming the role of the servant. He will wash the grimiest part of your life.

If you let him. The water of the Servant comes only when we confess that we are dirty. Only when we confess that we are caked with filth, that we have walked forbidden trails and followed the wrong paths.

We tend to be proud like Peter and resist. "I'm not that dirty, Jesus. Just sprinkle a few drops on me and I'll be fine."

What a lie! "If we say we have no sin, we are fooling ourselves, and the truth is not in us" (1 John 1:8).

We will never be cleansed until we confess we are dirty. We will never be pure until we admit we are filthy. And we will never be able to wash the feet of those who have hurt us until we allow Jesus, the one we have hurt, to wash ours.

You see, that is the secret of forgiveness. You will never forgive anyone more than God has already forgiven you. Only by letting him wash your feet can you have strength to wash those of another.

Still hard to imagine? Is it still hard to consider the thought of forgiving the one who hurt you?

If so, go one more time to the room. Watch Jesus as he goes from disciple to disciple. Can you see him? Can you hear the water splash? Can you hear him shuffle on the floor to the next person? Good. Keep that image.

John 13:12 says, "When he had finished washing their feet . . ."

Please note, he *finished* washing their feet. That means he left no one out. Why is that important? Because that also means he washed the feet of Judas. Jesus washed the feet of his betrayer. He gave his traitor equal attention. In just a few hours Judas's feet would guide the Roman guard to Jesus. But at this moment they are caressed by Christ.

That's not to say it was easy for Jesus.

That's not to say it is easy for you.

That is to say that God will never call you to do what he hasn't already done.

I am the bread that gives life.

John 6:35

The Bread of Life
The God Who Feeds My Soul

WHAT BREAD IS to hunger, Jesus claims to be for the soul.

Travel to almost any country and sit in any restaurant and they'll serve you bread. Bread is a staple. If the poor have nothing, they have bread. If the rich have everything, they still have bread. Bread is not a regional food nor a national dish. No country claims to be the exclusive source of bread. It may be in the form of a tortilla in Mexico or a bagel in New York, but bread is available everywhere. So is Christ. He is not bound by boundaries. No country claims him. No region owns him. No nation monopolizes him. He is everywhere at the same time. Universally available.

Bread is eaten daily. Some fruits are available only in season. Some drinks are made only at holidays. Not so with bread. And not so with Jesus. He should be brought to our table every day. We let him nourish our hearts, not just in certain months or on special events, but daily.

Bread is served in many forms. It's toasted, jellied, buttered, flattened, and grilled. It can be a sandwich, sweet roll, hot-dog bun, croissant, or dinner roll. Bread can meet many needs. So can Jesus. He adapts himself to meet our needs. He has a word for the lonely as well as for the popular. He has help for the physically ill and the emotionally ill. If your vision is clear, he can help you. If your vision is cloudy, he can help you. Jesus can meet each need.

Can you see why Jesus called himself the Bread of Life?

I can think of one other similarity. Consider how bread is made. Think about the process. Wheat grows in the field, then it is cut down, winnowed, and ground into flour. It passes through the fire of the oven and is then distributed around the world. Only by this process does bread become bread. Each step is essential. Eliminate the plant, and you have no wheat. Eliminate the winnowing, and you have no flour. Eliminate the fire, and you have no product. Eliminate the distribution, and you have no satisfaction. Each step is essential.

Now, consider Jesus. He grew up as a "small plant before the LORD" (Isa. 53:2). One of millions of boys on the planet. One of thousands in Israel. One of dozens in Nazareth. Indistinguishable from the person down the street or the child in the next chair. Had you seen him as a youngster, you wouldn't have thought he was the Son of God. You might have thought him polite or courteous or diligent, but God on earth? Not a chance. He was just a boy. One of hundreds. Like a staff of wheat in the wheat field.

But like wheat, he was cut down. Like chaff he was pounded and beaten. "He was wounded for the wrong we did; he was crushed for the evil we did" (Isa. 53:5). And like bread he passed through the fire. On the cross he passed though the fire of God's anger, not because of his sin, but because of ours. "The LORD has put on him the punishment for all the evil we have done" (Isa. 53:6).

Jesus experienced each part of the process of making bread: the growing, the pounding, the firing. And just as each is necessary for bread, each was also necessary for Christ to become the bread of life. "The Christ must suffer these things before he enters his glory" (Luke 24:26).

The next part of the process, the distribution, Christ leaves with us. We are the distributors. We can't force people to eat the bread, but we can make sure they have it. Yet, for some reason we are reluctant to do so. It's much easier to stay in the bakery than to get into the truck. As the following parable illustrates, we may not even know how to give the bread when someone requests it.

The Beggar and the Bread

A beggar came and sat before me. "I want bread," he said.

"How wise you are," I assured him. "Bread is what you need. And you have come to the right bakery." So I pulled my cookbook down from my shelf and began to tell him all I knew about bread.

I spoke of flour and wheat, of grain and barley. My knowledge impressed even me as I cited the measurements and recipe. When I looked up, I was surprised to see he wasn't smiling. "I just want bread," he said.

"How wise you are." I applauded his choice. "Follow me, and I'll show you our bakery." Down the hallowed halls I guided him, pausing to point out the rooms where the dough is prepared and the ovens where the bread is baked.

"No one has such facilities. We have bread for every need. But here is the best part," I proclaimed as I pushed open two swinging doors. "This is our room of inspiration." I knew he was moved as we stepped into the auditorium full of stained-glass windows.

The beggar didn't speak. I understood his silence. With my arm around his shoulder, I whispered, "It overwhelms me as well." I then leaped to the podium and struck my favorite pose behind the lectern. "People come from miles to hear me speak. Once a week my workers gather, and I read to them the recipe from the cookbook of life."

By now the beggar had taken a seat on the front row. I knew what he wanted. "Would you like to hear me?"

"No," he said, "but I would like some bread."

"How wise you are," I replied. And I led him to the front door of the bakery. "What I have to say next is very important," I told him as we stood outside. "Up and down this street you will find many bakeries. But take heed; they don't serve the true bread. I know of one who adds two spoons of salt rather than one. I know of another whose oven is three degrees too hot. They may call it bread," I warned, "but it's not according to the book."

The beggar turned and began walking away. "Don't you want bread?" I asked him.

He stopped, looked back at me, and shrugged, "I guess I lost my appetite."

I shook my head and returned to my office. "What a shame," I said to myself. "The world just isn't hungry for true bread anymore."

I don't know what is more incredible: that God packages the bread of life in the wrapper of a country carpenter or that he gives us the keys to the delivery truck. Both moves seem pretty risky. The carpenter did his part, however. And who knows—we may just learn to do ours.

*He had always loved those who were his own in
the world, and he loved them all the way to the end.*

John 13:1

Give thanks to the LORD *because he is good.
His love continues forever.*

Psalm 136:1

For Longer Than Forever
The God Who Loves Boldly

GOD, I HAVE a question: Why do you love your children? I don't want to sound irreverent, but only heaven knows how much pain we've brought you. Why do you tolerate us? You give us every breath we breathe, but do we thank you? You give us bodies beyond duplication, but do we praise you?

Seldom.

We complain about the weather. We bicker about our toys. We argue over who gets which continent and who has the best gender. Not a second passes when someone, somewhere, doesn't use your name to curse a hammered thumb or a bad call by the umpire. (As if it were your fault.)

You fill the world with food, but we blame you for hunger. You keep the earth from tilting and the arctics from thawing, but we accuse you of unconcern. You give us blue skies, and we demand rain. You give rain, and we demand sun. (As if we knew what was best anyway.)

We give more applause to a brawny ball-carrier than we do to the God who made us. We sing more songs to the moon than to the Christ who saved us. We are a gnat on the tail of one elephant in a galaxy of Africas, and yet we demand that you find us a parking place when we ask. And if you don't give us what we want, we say you don't exist. (As if our opinion matters.)

We pollute the world you loan us. We mistreat the bodies you gave us. We ignore the Word you sent us. And we killed the Son you became. We are spoiled babies who take and kick and pout and blaspheme.

You have every reason to abandon us.

I sure would! I would wash my hands of the whole mess and start over on Mars. But do you?

I see the answer in the rising of the sun. I hear the answer in the crashing of the waves. I feel the answer in the skin of a child.

Father, your love never ceases. Never. Though we spurn you, ignore you, disobey you, you will not change. Our evil cannot diminish your love. Our goodness cannot increase it. Our faith does not earn it anymore than our stupidity jeopardizes it. You don't love us less if we fail. You don't love us more if we succeed.

Your love never ceases.

How do we explain it?

Perhaps the answer is found in yet another question.

Moms: Why do you love your newborn? I know, I know; it's a silly question, but indulge me. Why do you?

For months this baby has brought you pain. She (or he!) made you break out in pimples and waddle like a duck. Because of her you craved sardines and crackers and threw up in the morning. She punched you in the tummy. She occupied space that wasn't hers and ate food she didn't fix.

You kept her warm. You kept her safe. You kept her fed. But did she say thank you?

Are you kidding? She's no more out of the womb than she starts to cry! The room is too cold, the blanket is too rough, the nurse is too mean. And who does she want? Mom.

Don't you ever get a break? I mean, who has been doing the work the last nine months? Why can't Dad take over? But no, Dad won't do. The baby wants Mom.

She didn't even tell you she was coming. She just came. And what a coming! She rendered you a barbarian. You screamed. You swore. You bit bullets and tore the sheets. And now look at you. Your back aches. Your head pounds. Your body is drenched in sweat. Every muscle strained and stretched.

You should be angry, but are you?

Far from it. On your face is a for-longer-than-forever love. She has done nothing for you; yet you love her. She's brought pain to your body and nausea to your morning, yet you treasure her. Her face is wrinkled and her eyes are dim, yet all you can talk about are her good looks and bright future. She's going to wake you up every night for the next six weeks, but that doesn't matter. I can see it on your face. You're crazy about her.

Why?

Why does a mother love her newborn? Because the baby is hers? Even more. Because the baby is her. Her blood. Her flesh. Her sinew and spine. Her hope. Her legacy. It bothers her not that the baby gives nothing. She knows a newborn is helpless, weak. She knows babies don't ask to come into this world.

And God knows we didn't either.

We are his idea. We are his. His face. His eyes. His hands. His touch. We are him. Look deeply into the face of every human being on earth, and you will see his likeness. Though some appear to be distant relatives, they are not. God has no cousins, only children.

We are, incredibly, the body of Christ. And though we may not act like our Father, there is no greater truth than this: We are his. Unalterably. He loves us. Undyingly. Nothing can separate us from the love of Christ (see Rom. 8:38–39).

Had God not said those words, I would be a fool to write them. But since he did, I'm a fool not to believe them. Nothing can separate us from the love of Christ . . . but how difficult it is for some to embrace this truth.

You think you've committed an act that places you outside his love. A treason. A betrayal. An aborted promise. You think he would love you more if you hadn't done it, right? You think he would love you more if you did more, right? You think if you were better his love would be deeper, right?

Wrong. Wrong. Wrong.

God's love is not human. His love is not normal. His love sees your sin and loves you still. Does he approve of your error? No. Do you need to repent? Yes. But do you repent for his sake or yours? Yours. His ego needs no apology. His love needs no bolstering.

And he could not love you more than he does right now.

When Jesus said, "I am he," they moved back and fell to the ground.

John 18:6

Lessons from the Garden

The God Who Reclaims the Sacred

MY FATHER TAUGHT me the lesson early: Don't create havoc in the garden. You can play ball in the yard. You can have races in the alley. You can build a fort in the tree. But the garden? Leave it alone.

It was a small garden, about the size of a walk-in closet. We grew nothing exotic, except for some mint. We'd soak the leaves in our summer tea. Though the vegetables were tasty, we didn't need to grow them. We could have bought them at the market. So why did Dad insist on having a garden?

He loved to see life. And a garden is a place of life, a place where buds explode and plants push back the soil. A place of turnips and tulips and tomato plants. A place worthy of love and protection. Flowers are fragile. Plants are precious. So yank the weeds and scatter the varmints. Put up a fence. Grow a hedge. Make a scarecrow.

"Son, whatever you do, don't go trampling around in the garden."

I hate to think I have anything in common with the devil, but I guess I do. Satan learned the same lesson: Don't mess around with a garden—especially a garden that belongs to the Father.

The Bible is the story of two gardens. Eden and Gethsemane. In the first, Adam took a fall. In the second, Jesus took a stand. In the first, God sought Adam. In the second, Jesus sought God. In Eden,

Adam hid from God. In Gethsemane, Jesus emerged from the tomb. In Eden, Satan led Adam to a tree that led to his death. From Gethsemane, Jesus went to a tree that led to our life.

Satan was never invited to the Garden of Eden. He did not belong there. He was not wanted there. He slithered as a snake into God's garden and infected God's children.

That's all he's done since. Hasn't he entered a few of your holy gardens?

We even call it "holy matrimony." The word altar implies the presence of God. Marriage was God's idea. The first wedding occurred in the first garden. But that doesn't make any difference to the devil. He snakes his way into every home with one desire—to destroy.

Sexual intimacy is God's gift. Virginity is a rose plucked from the garden, given by God and intended to be shared with your forever partner. Satan mocks such loyalty. He is the father of incest and abuse. He is the author of immorality. He is the pimp of the garden.

We give sacred oaths and make solemn promises. We vow to be a good parent, a true companion, and a loyal friend. But Satan's head turns when he hears a pledge. "We'll see about that," the father of lies smirks.

In God's eyes, a child is holy. The innocence of youth, the freshness of childhood, the joy of an infant. There was never a moment when Jesus turned away a child. But there has never been a child Satan didn't despise. He was killing babies to kill Moses. He was destroying infants to destroy the Christ. His tactics haven't changed. Millions of babies are still aborted; thousands of children are abused. Jesus said of Satan, "He was a murderer from the beginning" (John 8:44).

Is there a realm untouched by Satan? Is there a place unscarred by his sword? The church? The government? Children? Purity? Promises?

And you! And me! We are called to be holy. We were made to be holy. Set apart for his good work. We are the prized flowers of the garden. But is there one person who has not felt the foot of the intruder?

What Satan did in Eden, he does today. For that reason we need to know that what Jesus did in Gethsemane, he does today. He reclaims the holy. He will not long sit silent while Satan strip-mines the sacred. At the right moment Jesus stands and speaks. And when he stands and speaks, Satan stumbles and is silent.

Exactly what happened in Gethsemane.

John tells us that "Judas came there with a group of soldiers and some guards from the leading priests and Pharisees" (John 18:3). A bit of study reveals that Satan has masterminded a mighty coup. He has enlisted the muscle of each significant force of the drama—the Romans, the Jews, and the apostles.

First he has a "group of soldiers." The Greek word is *speira*. It has three possible meanings. It can signify a Roman cohort of three hundred men. It can refer to a cavalry and infantry totaling nineteen hundred soldiers. Or it can describe a detachment known as a *maniple*, which contained two hundred men.[1]

Amazing. I always had the impression that a handful of soldiers arrested Jesus. I was wrong. At minimum two hundred soldiers were dispatched to deal with a single carpenter and his eleven friends!

Also present were "some guards." This was the temple police. They were assigned to guard the holiest place during the busiest time of the year. They must have been among Israel's finest.

And then there was Judas. One of the inner circle. Not only had Satan recruited the Romans and the Jews, he had infiltrated the cabinet. Hell must have been rejoicing. There was no way Jesus could escape. Satan sealed every exit. His lieutenants anticipated every move, except one.

Jesus had no desire to run. He had no intent of escape. He hadn't come to the garden to retreat. What they found among the trees was no coward; what they found was a conqueror.

Note the dialogue that ensued:

> Knowing everything that would happen to him, Jesus went out and asked, "Who is it you are looking for?"

They answered, "Jesus from Nazareth."

"I am he," Jesus said. (Judas, the one who turned against Jesus, was standing there with them.) When Jesus said, "I am he," they moved back and fell to the ground.

Jesus asked them again, "Who is it you are looking for?"

They said, "Jesus of Nazareth."

"I told you that I am he," Jesus said. "So if you are looking for me, let the others go" (John 18:4–8).

Remarkable. They stand only a few feet from his face and don't recognize him. Not even Judas realizes who stands before them. What a truth. Seeing Jesus is more than a matter of the eyes; it is a matter of the heart. The enemy is next to Jesus and doesn't realize it.

He reveals himself. "I am he." His voice flicks the first domino, and down they tumble. Were the moment not so solemn it would be comic. These are the best soldiers with Satan's finest plan; yet one word from Jesus, and they fall down! The Roman guard becomes the Keystone Cops. Two hundred fighting men collapse into a noisy pile of shields, swords, and lamps. Don't miss the symbolism here: When Jesus speaks, Satan falls.

Doesn't matter who the evil one has recruited. Doesn't matter if he has infiltrated the government. Doesn't matter if he has seduced the temple. Doesn't matter if he has enlisted one of the original, handpicked apostles. The best of Satan melts as wax before the presence of Christ.

Jesus has to ask them again whom they seek. "Who are you after?"

When they answer that they are looking for Jesus of Nazareth, he instructs them, "So if you are looking for me, let the others go."

What is this? Jesus commanding them! A Jew instructing a Roman? A renegade directing the temple guard? We turn to the commander, expecting a reply. We look at Judas, awaiting his retort. We listen, expecting someone to announce, "You're not the one in charge here, Nazarene! We'll take whoever we want."

But not only are they silent, they are obedient. The apostles are set free.

Many players appear on the stage of Gethsemane. Judas and his betrayal. Peter and his sword. The disciples and their fears. The soldiers and their weapons. And though these are crucial, they aren't instrumental. The encounter is not between Jesus and the soldiers; it is between God and Satan. Satan dares to enter yet another garden, but God stands and Satan hasn't a prayer.

Don't miss the message:

> Our fight is not against people on earth but against the rulers and authorities and the powers of this world's darkness, against the spiritual powers of evil in the heavenly world (Eph. 6:12).

> The Son of God came for this purpose: to destroy the devil's work (1 John 3:8).

Don't miss the promises:

Satan falls in the presence of Christ. One word from his lips, and the finest army in the world collapsed.

Satan is silent in the proclamation of Christ. Not once did the enemy speak without Jesus' invitation. Before Christ, Satan has nothing to say.

Satan is powerless against the protection of Christ. "I have not lost any of the ones you gave me" (John 18:9).

When Jesus says he will keep you safe, he means it. Hell will have to get through him to get to you. Jesus is able to protect you. When he says he will get you home, he will get you home.

Let me conclude this chapter with an important question. Has Satan invaded a garden of your life? Has he profaned a holy part of your world? Your marriage? Your purity? Your honesty? Has he taken away from you a rose God gave? If so, let Jesus claim it back. Today. Now. Before you turn the page.

Forgive me for sounding urgent, but I am. Satan has no authority over you. If he has invaded a garden of your life, then invite Jesus to reclaim it. Open the gate to God. He will enter and do what he did at Gethsemane. He will pray, and he will protect.

Why don't you do that?

Don't know how? It's easy. I'll help you. Let's pray. You and me. I'll show you the way; you fill in the blanks.

> Precious Father, I praise your name. You have reclaimed so much in my life. I was lost, and you found me. I was confused, and you guided me. I had nothing to offer, but still you loved me.
>
> I confess that I still need help. I have a part of my life that needs your touch. Satan is battling for a garden in my heart. Don't let him win. Drive him out. He is a liar and has been since the beginning. Please defeat him. I'll give you the glory.
>
> Father, here is the area where I need your strength
>
> _____.

(And here is the place where I step out. I'll leave you and God to talk over the details. I'll be waiting for you in the next chapter.)

Don't let your hearts be troubled. Trust in God,
and trust in me.

John 14:1

What to Do with Birthdays
The God of Grave Victory

THE COMMENTS BEGAN a couple of months ago.

> "Getting close to the top there, Max? Be careful. You pick up speed going downhill."

> "Almost there, eh, Max? Won't be long before you'll stop combing your hair and start arranging it."

Thirty days out, the word started to spread (so did my waist). Reminders became more frequent.

> "Look at it this way. All your life you've been taught to respect your elders. Now you don't have to respect anyone."

> "Don't worry, Max. Old age isn't bad when you consider the alternative."

This week the phone calls started to arrive.

> "I don't know whether to send condolences or congratulations."

"Able to make it out of bed this morning?" my brother asked today.

Actually I got out of bed earlier than normal this morning. On a typical birthday I might have waved off my morning jog and stayed in bed. But this isn't a typical birthday. And the thought of staying in bed never entered my mind. The thought of jogging an extra mile did, but not the thought of sleeping late.

It's the big one. The fortieth. In defiance of age, I stepped onto the dark streets and ran. I wanted to see what a forty-year-old jogger feels like. Know what I learned? He feels like a thirty-nine-year-old jogger.

But even though I feel the same as I did yesterday, my driver's license reminds me I am forty. They say that life begins at forty. But so do bad eyesight, arthritis, and the habit of telling the same joke three times to the same person.

Lucille Ball said the secret of staying young is to live honestly, eat slowly, and lie about your age. Easier said than done. It's hard to lie about the obvious. When you are young you make a lot of faces in the mirror. When you are old the mirror gets even. But I tell myself that turning forty isn't too bad; next to a Galapagos turtle I'm still a child.

I've gotten several laughs out of the comments that have come my way. Thought you might enjoy a few:

> "You know you are getting older when you try to straighten out the wrinkles in your socks only to find you aren't wearing any."

> "At twenty we don't care what the world thinks of us; at thirty we start to worry about what the world thinks of us; at forty we realize the world isn't thinking of us at all."

> "I've gotten to the age where I need my false teeth and hearing aid before I can ask where I left my glasses."

> "Forty is when you stop patting yourself on the back and start patting yourself under the chin."

I'll leave it to Dave Barry to sum it up:

> As a person starts reaching this milestone (your fortieth birthday) you need to take time to learn about the biological changes that are taking place within your body, so that you will be better able to understand and cope with the inevitable and completely natural elements of the aging process—the minor aches, pains, dental problems, intestinal malfunctions, muscle deterioration, emotional instability, memory lapses, hearing and vision loss, impotence, seizures, growths, prostate problems, greatly reduced limb function, massive coronary failure, death and, of course, painful hemorrhoid swelling—that can make up this exciting adventure we call "middle age."[1]

Growing older. Aging. We laugh about it, and we groan about it. We resist it, but we can't stop it. And with the chuckles and wrinkles come some serious thoughts and questions about what happens when we die. Is death when we go to sleep? Or is death when we finally wake up?

As a minister, I'm often asked to speak at funerals. I no longer have to ask the family what they want me to say; I already know. Oh, I may have to ask a question or two about the deceased, and that I do, but I don't ask them about what they want me to say. I know.

They want to hear what God says about death. They want to hear how God would answer their questions about the life hereafter. They don't want my opinion; nor do they want the thoughts of a philosopher or the research of a scientist. They want to know what God says. If Jesus were here, at the head of this casket, in the middle of this cemetery, what would he say?

And so under the canopy of sorrow, I give God's words. I share the eulogy Jesus gave for himself. The disciples did not know it was his farewell address. No one did, but it was. He knew he had just witnessed his final sunset. He knew death would come with the morning. So he spoke about death. Here is how he began.

Don't let your hearts be troubled. Trust in God, and trust in me. There are many rooms in my Father's house; I would not tell you this if it were not true. I am going there to prepare a place for you. After I go and prepare a place for you, I will come back and take you to be with me so that you may be where I am (John 14:1–4).

What kind of statement is that? Trust me with your death. When you face the tomb, don't be troubled—trust me! You get the impression that to God the grave is a no-brainer. He speaks as casually as the mechanic who says to a worried client, "Sure, the engine needs an overhaul, but don't worry. I can do it." For us it's an ordeal. For him it's no big deal.

The other night I did something that every parent has done dozens of times. I carried my daughter to bed. Five-year-old Sara fell asleep on the floor, and I picked her up, carried her up the stairs, and put her in bed. Why? I knew it was time for her to rest, and I knew that rest was better up there than down here.

Doesn't God do the same? Doesn't he, knowing more than we, carry us to the place of rest he created? For God, death is no tragedy. In God's economy, the termination of the body is the beginning of life.

Can you imagine if Sara's sisters objected to my decision to carry her upstairs? "Don't take her. We'll miss her. Please keep her here so we will all be together."

How would I answer? "Oh, but she'll rest so much better in the room I have prepared for her. Besides, you'll be coming up yourselves soon."

By calling us home, God is doing what any father would do. He is providing a better place to rest. A place he has "prepared for us." Heaven is not mass-produced; it is tailor-made.

Sometime ago I indulged and ordered two shirts from a tailor. I selected the cloth. The tailor measured my body. And several weeks later, I received two shirts made especially for me. There is a big difference between these two shirts and the other shirts in my closet. The tailored shirts were made with me in mind. The other shirts were made for any hundred thousand or so males my size. But not these two. They were made just for me.

As a result, they fit! They don't bulge. They don't choke. They are just right. Such is the promise of heaven. It was made with us in mind. Elsewhere Jesus invites us to "receive the kingdom God has prepared for you since the world was made" (Matt. 25:34).

The problem with this world is that it doesn't fit. Oh, it will do for now, but it isn't tailor-made. We were made to live with God, but on earth we live by faith. We were made to live forever, but on this earth we live but for a moment. We were made to live holy lives, but this world is stained by sin.

This world wears like a borrowed shirt. Heaven, however, will fit like one tailor-made.

By the way, I've often thought it curious how few people Jesus raised from the dead. He healed hundreds and fed thousands, but as far as we know he only raised three: the daughter of Jairus, the boy near Nain, and Lazarus. Why so few? Could it be because he knew he'd be doing them no favors? Could it be because he couldn't get any volunteers? Could it be that once someone is there, the last place they want to return to is here?

We must trust God. We must trust not only that he does what is best but that he knows what is ahead. Ponder these words of Isaiah 57:1–2: "The good men perish; the godly die before their time and no one seems to care or wonder why. No one seems to realize that God is taking them away from the evil days ahead. For the godly who die shall rest in peace" (TLB).

My, what a thought. God is taking them away from the evil days ahead. Could death be God's grace? Could the funeral wreath be God's safety ring? Why does an eight-year-old die of cancer? Why is a young mother taken from her children? As horrible as the grave may be, could it be God's protection from the future?

Trust in God, Jesus urges, and trust in me.

Several years ago I heard then Vice President George Bush speak at a prayer breakfast. He told of his trip to Russia to represent the United States at the funeral of Leonid Brezhnev. The funeral was as precise and stoic as the communist regime. No tears were seen, and no emotion displayed. With one exception. Mr. Bush told how Brezhnev's widow was the last person to witness the body before the coffin was closed. For several seconds she stood at his side and then reached down and performed the sign of the cross on her husband's chest.

In the hour of her husband's death, she went not to Lenin, not to Karl Marx, not to Khrushchev. In the hour of death she turned to a Nazarene carpenter who had lived two thousand years ago and who dared to claim: "Don't let your hearts be troubled. Trust in God, and trust in me."[2]

So what do we do with birthdays? As much as we'd like to avoid them, we can't. Pretty soon the candles cost as much as the cake. And as much as we'd like to think we are exempt from the grave, we aren't. So rather than avoid them, welcome them! Welcome them as mile-markers that remind you that you aren't home yet, but you're closer than you've ever been.

When I go away, I will send the Helper to you. If I do not go away, the Helper will not come. When the Helper comes, he will prove to the people of the world the truth about sin, about being right with God, and about judgment.

John 16:7–9

10

Music for the Dance
The God Who Sends the Song

LET'S IMAGINE THAT you want to learn to dance. Being the rational, cerebral person you are, you go to a bookstore and buy a book on dancing. After all, a book helped you learn to program a computer, and a book taught you accounting—surely a book can teach you how to shuffle your feet.

You take the book home and get to work. You do everything it says. The book says sway; you sway. The book says shuffle; you shuffle. The book says spin; you spin. You even cut out paper shoe patterns and place them around the living-room floor so you'll know where to step.

Finally, you think you've got it, and you invite your wife to come in and watch. You hold the book open and follow the instructions step by step. You even read the words aloud so she'll know that you've done your homework. "Lean with your right shoulder," and so you lean. "Now step with your right foot," and so you step. "Turn slowly to the left," and so you do.

You continue to read, then dance, read, then dance, until the dance is completed. You plop exhausted on the couch, look at your wife, and proclaim, "I executed it perfectly."

"You executed it, all right," she sighs. "You killed it."

"What?"

"You forgot the most important part. Where is the music?"

Music?

You never thought about music. You remembered the book. You learned the rules. You laid out the pattern. But you forgot the music.

"Do it again," she says, putting in a CD. "This time don't worry about the steps; just follow the music."

She extends her hand and the music begins. The next thing you know, you are dancing—and you don't even have the book.

We Christians are prone to follow the book while ignoring the music. We master the doctrine, outline the chapters, memorize the dispensations, debate the rules, and stiffly step down the dance floor of life with no music in our hearts. We measure each step, calibrate each turn, and flop into bed each night exhausted from another day of dancing by the book.

Dancing with no music is tough stuff.

Jesus knew that. For that reason, on the night before his death he introduced the disciples to the song maker of the Trinity, the Holy Spirit.

> When I go away I will send the Helper to you. If I do not go away, the Helper will not come. When the Helper comes, he will prove to the people of the world the truth about sin, about being right with God, and about judgment (John 16:7–9).

If I were to ask you to describe your heavenly Father, you'd give me a response. If I were to ask you to tell me what Jesus did for you, you'd likely give a cogent answer. But if I were to ask about the role of the Holy Spirit in your life . . . ? Eyes would duck. Throats would be cleared. And it would soon be obvious that of the three persons of the Godhead, the Holy Spirit is the one we understand the least.

Perhaps the most common mistake made regarding the Spirit is perceiving him as a power but not a person, a force with no identity. Such is not true. The Holy Spirit is a person.

The world cannot accept *him*, because it does not see him or know *him*. But you know *him*, because *he* lives with you and *he* will be in you (John 14:17, emphasis mine).

The Holy Spirit is not an "it." He is a person. He has knowledge (1 Cor. 2:11). He has a will (1 Cor. 12:11). He has a mind (Rom. 8:27). He has affections (Rom. 15:30). You can lie to him (Acts 5:3–4). You can insult him (Heb. 10:29). You can grieve him (Eph. 4:30).

The Holy Spirit is not an impersonal force. He is not Popeye's spinach or the surfer's wave. He is God within you to help you. In fact John calls him the Helper.

Envision a father helping his son learn to ride a bicycle, and you will have a partial picture of the Holy Spirit. The father stays at the son's side. He pushes the bike and steadies it if the boy starts to tumble. The Spirit does that for us; he stays our step and strengthens our stride. Unlike the father, however, he never leaves. He is with us to the end of the age.

What does the Spirit do?

He comforts the saved. "When I go away, I will send the Helper to you" (John 16:7).

He convicts the lost. "When the Helper comes, he will prove to the people of the world the truth about sin, about being right with God, and about judgment" (John 16:8).

He conveys the truth. "I have many more things to say to you, but they are too much for you now. When the Spirit of truth comes, he will lead you into all truth" (John 16:12).

Is John saying we don't need the book in order to dance? Of course not; he helped write it. Emotion without knowledge is as dangerous as knowledge without emotion. God seeks a balance. "God is spirit, and those who worship him must worship in spirit and truth" (John 4:24).

What is essential is that you know the music is in you. "If Christ is in you, then the Spirit gives you life" (Rom. 8:10). You don't need a formula to hear it. I don't have a four-step plan to help you know it. What I do have is his promise that the helper would come to comfort, convict, and convey.

So think about it; have you ever been comforted? Has God ever brought you peace when the world brought you pain? Then you heard the music.

Have you ever been convicted? Have you ever sensed a stab of sorrow for your actions? Then you've been touched by the Holy Spirit.

Or have you ever understood a new truth? Or seen an old principle in a new way? The light comes on. Your eyes pop open. "Aha, now I understand." Ever happen to you? If so, that was the Holy Spirit conveying to you a new truth.

What do you know? He's been working in your life already.

By the way, for those of us who spent years trying to do God's job, that is great news. It's much easier to raise the sail than row the boat. And it's a lot easier getting people to join the dance when God is playing the music.

I am the good shepherd. The good shepherd gives his life for his sheep. The worker who is paid to keep the sheep is different from the shepherd who owns them.

John 10:11–12

I am the good shepherd. I know my sheep as the Father knows me.

John 10:14–15

A Different Kind of Hero
The God Who Knows Your Name

BEHOLD A HERO of the west: the cowboy.

He rears his horse to a stop on the rim of the canyon. He shifts his weight in his saddle, weary from the cattle trail. One finger pushes his hat up on his head. One jerk of the kerchief reveals a sun-leathered face.

A thousand head of cattle pass behind him. A thousand miles of trail lie before him. A thousand women would love to hold him. But none do. None will. He lives to drive cattle, and he drives cattle to live. He is honest in poker and quick with a gun. Hard riding. Slow talking. His best friend is his horse, and his strength is his grit.

He needs no one. He is a cowboy. The American hero.

Behold a hero in the Bible: the shepherd.

On the surface he appears similar to the cowboy. He, too, is rugged. He sleeps where the jackals howl and works where the wolves prowl. Never off duty. Always alert. Like the cowboy, he makes his roof the stars and the pasture his home.

But that is where the similarities end.

The shepherd loves his sheep. It's not that the cowboy doesn't appreciate the cow; it's just that he doesn't know the animal. He doesn't even want to. Have you ever seen a picture of a cowboy caressing a cow? Have you ever seen a shepherd caring for a sheep? Why the difference?

Simple. The cowboy leads the cow to slaughter. The shepherd leads the sheep to be shorn. The cowboy wants the meat of the cow. The shepherd wants the wool of the sheep. And so they treat the animals differently.

The cowboy drives the cattle. The shepherd leads the sheep.

A herd has a dozen cowboys. A flock has one shepherd.

The cowboy wrestles, brands, herds, and ropes. The shepherd leads, guides, feeds, and anoints.

The cowboy knows the name of the trail hands. The shepherd knows the name of the sheep.

The cowboy whoops and hollers at the cows. The shepherd calls each sheep by name.

Aren't we glad Christ didn't call himself the Good Cowboy? But some do perceive God that way. A hard-faced, square-jawed ranch-hand from heaven who drives his church against its will to places it doesn't want to go.

But that's a wrong image. Jesus called himself the Good Shepherd. The Shepherd who knows his sheep by name and lays down his life for them. The Shepherd who protects, provides, and possesses his sheep. The Bible is replete with this picture of God.

"The Lord is my shepherd" (Ps. 23:1).

"We are your people, the sheep of your flock" (Ps. 79:13).

"Shepherd of Israel, listen to us. You lead the people of Joseph like a flock" (Ps. 80:1).

"He is our God and we are the people he takes care of and the sheep that he tends" (Ps. 95:7).

"He made us, and we belong to him; we are his people, the sheep he tends" (Ps. 100:3).

The imagery is carried over to the New Testament.

He is the shepherd who will risk his life to save the one straying sheep (see Luke 15:4).

He has pity on people because they are like sheep without a shepherd (see Matt. 9:36).

His disciples are his flock (see Luke 12:32.)

When the shepherd is attacked, the sheep are scattered (see Matt. 26:31).

He is the shepherd of the souls of men (see 1 Peter 2:25).

He is the great shepherd of the sheep (see Heb. 13:20).

Eighty percent of Jesus' listeners made their living off of the land. Many were shepherds. They lived on the mesa with the sheep. No flock ever grazed without a shepherd, and no shepherd was ever off duty. When sheep wandered, the shepherd found them. When they fell, he carried them. When they were hurt, he healed them.

Sheep aren't smart. They tend to wander into running creeks for water, then their wool grows heavy and they drown. They need a shepherd to lead them to "calm water" (Ps. 23:2). They have no natural defense—no claws, no horns, no fangs. They are helpless. Sheep need a shepherd with a "rod and . . . walking stick" (Ps. 23:4) to protect them. They have no sense of direction. They need someone to lead them "on paths that are right" (Ps. 23:3).

So do we. We, too, tend to be swept away by waters we should have avoided. We have no defense against the evil lion who prowls about seeking who he might devour. We, too, get lost. "We all have wandered away like sheep; each of us has gone his own way" (Isa. 53:6).

We need a shepherd. We don't need a cowboy to herd us; we need a shepherd to care for us and to guide us.

And we have one. One who knows us by name.

I don't need to tell you why this is so important, do I? You know. Like me, you've probably been in a situation where someone forgot your name. Perhaps a situation where no one knew who you were—or even cared.

Not long ago my assistant, Karen Hill, underwent surgery. When she awoke in the recovery room, she could hear a fellow patient groaning. She heard a well-meaning nurse comforting him. "Settle down, Tom," she said. "Settle down." But still he moaned. The nurse returned. "It's all right, Tom. Just go with the pain." He was quiet for a few moments but then began groaning again. "It's okay, Tom. You'll be fine." Finally the patient spoke. With a low, painful voice he said, "My name's not Tom."

There was a moment of silence as the nurse picked up his chart. Then she said, "It's all right, Harry; it's all right."

It's never easy to be in a place where no one knows your name, but few of us know this as much as John Doe No. 24. His story, as recorded by the Associated Press, reads like this:

UNKNOWN SINCE '45,
JOHN DOE TAKES HIS
SECRET TO THE GRAVE

JACKSONVILLE, ILL.

The mystery of John Doe No. 24 outlived him. There were few clues when he was found, wandering the streets of Jacksonville in 1945, a deaf, blind teenager.

Since he was unable to speak and his relatives could not be found, he was placed in an institution. He became John Doe No. 24 because he was the twenty-fourth unidentified man in the state's mental health system. Officials believe he was sixty-four when he died of a stroke at the Sharon Oaks nursing home in Peoria.

John Doe's caretakers believe diabetes made him lose his sight, and records indicate he was severely retarded. But workers remember a proud man, more intelligent than the standard tests showed. They remember the tantalizing hints to his identity—the way he would scrawl "Lewis" and his pantomimed wild accounts of foot-stomping jazz bars and circus parades. "It was so obvious from what he panto-mimed that he had quite a life at one time," said Kim Cornwell, a caseworker. "Like my grandfather, he could probably tell funny stories. We just couldn't reach out enough to get them." . . .

He had a straw hat he loved to wear and he took a back-pack with his collection of rings, glasses and silverware with him everywhere. At Christmas parties he danced to vibrations from the music. Last Christmas the staff bought him a harmonica. . . .

At a brief graveside service last Wednesday in Jacksonville, a woman asked if anyone had any words to say. No one did.[1]

Somewhere in the darkness of John Doe No. 24 there was a story. There was a name. There were memories of a mother who held him, a father who carried him. Behind those sightless eyes were eyes that could see the past, and all we can do is wonder, *What did they see? A kid with a cane pole on a muddy river? A wide-eyed youngster eating popcorn at a circus? A jazz band in New Orleans?*

No one will ever know. No one will know because he could never tell. He couldn't even speak his name. And on the day he died no one had words to say. What do you say when you bury a life no one knew?

It's easy to say this, but I wish I'd been there. I would have opened the Bible to the tenth chapter of the Gospel of John and read verse 3, "He calls his own sheep by name and leads them out."

It's not true that no one knew this man's name. God did . . . and God does. And it's wrong to say that this man never heard his name. Who knows how many times God spoke it to him through the years? In the silence. Through the dark. When we thought he couldn't hear, who is to say he wasn't hearing the only voice that matters?

The Good Shepherd knows each sheep by name. He's not a cowboy, and we aren't cattle. He doesn't brand us, and we're not on the way to the market. He guides, feeds, and anoints. And Word has it that he won't quit until we reach the homeland.

I give them eternal life, and they will never die,
and no one can steal them out of my hand.

John 10:28

Held by His Hands

The God Who Won't Let You Fall

I WOULD LIKE to confess a fall. I've kept it secret long enough. I can't deny the stumble; nor can I dismiss the truth. I fell. There were witnesses to my slip. They can tell you. Graciously, they have told no one. Out of concern for my reputation, they kept the event a secret. But it has been a secret long enough. The time has come for my mistake to be shared.

I lost my footing at a family camp.

My daughters and I chose to climb a wall—a simulated rock climb. The wall is made of wood with occasional rock-shaped fingerholds bolted into the surface. For safety, the climber wears a harness around his waist. The harness is attached to a rope that runs up through a pulley and then down into the hands of a guide who secures it as the climber climbs.

I gave it a go. What's a fifty-foot wall for a middle-aged author? I gave the guide the "thumbs-up" and began. The first half of the trip I did well. About midway, however, I began to get tired. These hands and feet are not accustomed to climbing.

With about twenty feet left to go, I honestly began to wonder if I would make it. I gave serious thought to telling the guide just to pull me up the rest of the way. My fingers were sore, and my legs were starting to tremble, and I was regretting every Big Mac I'd ever eaten, but the thought of surrender was lost in the cheers of my daughters who were already on the top.

"Come on, Dad. You can make it!"

So I gave it all I had. But all I had was not enough. My feet slipped, my hands slipped, and down I fell. I fell hard. But I didn't fall far. My guide had a firm hold on the rope. Because he was alert and because he was strong, my tumble lasted only a couple of seconds. I bounced and swung in the harness, suspended in midair. Everyone watching let out a sigh, and I gulped and resumed the climb.

Guess what I did when I made it to the top? Do you think I boasted? Do you think I bragged about conquering the wall? No way. I looked down at the one who kept me from falling. "Thanks, pal," I told him. I didn't pat myself on the back or raise my fist in triumph. I didn't ask everybody if they'd seen what I did. I did the only thing that was right; I said thanks to the one who held me.

Would that all my tumbles were so simple. So brief. So harmless. They haven't been. I've been known to let go of much more than imitation rocks. I've let go of promises and convictions. There have been times when my fingers slipped off the very stones of truth I treasure. And I can't tell you how many times I've expected to hit the bottom only to find myself suspended in midair, secured by a pair of nail-pierced hands.

"Try again," he urges. And so I resume.

You and I are on a great climb. The wall is high, and the stakes are higher. You took your first step the day you confessed Christ as the Son of God. He gave you his harness—the Holy Spirit. In your hands he placed a rope—his Word.

Your first steps were confident and strong, but with the journey came weariness, and with the height came fear. You lost your footing. You lost your focus. You lost your grip, and you fell. For a moment, which seemed like forever, you tumbled wildly. Out of control. Out of self-control. Disoriented. Dislodged. Falling.

But then the rope tightened, and the tumble ceased. You hung in the harness and found it to be strong. You grasped the rope and found it to be true. You looked at your guide and found Jesus securing your soul. With a sheepish confession, you smiled at him and he smiled at you, and the journey resumed.

Now you are wiser. You have learned to go slowly. You are careful. You are cautious, but you are also confident. You trust the rope. You rely on the harness. And though you can't see your guide, you know him. You know he is strong. You know he is able to keep you from falling.

And you know you are only a few more steps from the top. So whatever you do, don't quit. Though your falls are great, his strength is greater. You will make it. You will see the summit. You will stand at the top. And when you get there, the first thing you'll do is join with all the others who have made the climb and sing this verse:

"To him who is able to keep you from falling and to present you before his glorious presence without fault and with great joy—to the only God our Savior be glory, majesty, power and authority, through Jesus Christ our Lord, before all ages, now and forevermore! Amen" (Jude 24 NIV).

Carrying his own cross, Jesus went out to a place called The Place of the Skull. . . . There they crucified Jesus. They also crucified two other men, one on each side, with Jesus in the middle.

John 19:17

A Cinderella Story
The God Who Gave His Beauty Away

God between two thieves. Exactly the place he wants to be.

Three men on three crosses, a well-known scene. Even casual students of Christ are acquainted with the trio on Skull's Hill. We've pondered their sufferings and sketched their faces and analyzed their words.

But let's imagine this scene from another perspective. Rather than stand on ground level and look up, let's stand at the throne of God and look down. What does God see? What is the perspective of heaven? Does God see the timber and nails? Does God witness the torn flesh and spilt blood? Can heaven hear the mallet slam and the voices cry?

Certainly. But God sees much more. He sees his Son surrounded by sin and two thieves covered with sin. A shadow hangs over their spirits. The crowd cringes at the sight of the blood on their skin, but heaven laments over the darkness of their hearts. Earth pities the condition of their bodies. Heaven weeps over the condition of their souls.

I wonder if we can understand the impact our sin has in heaven. We get a clue in Revelation 3:16 when Jesus threatens to spit the lukewarm church out of his mouth. The verb literally means "to vomit." Their sin, excuse the phrase, made God want to puke. Their acts caused him, not just distaste, but disgust.

Haven't you felt the same? Haven't you witnessed the horror of a human act and wanted to throw up? On last night's news broadcast the story was told of a ten-year-old boy who'd been allegedly set afire by his father. The man had stuffed tissue down his son's T-shirt, covered the boy with lighter fluid, and set him aflame. Why? Because the boy had taken some of the father's food stamps.

Doesn't such a story disgust you? Make you angry? And if we, who are also sinners, have such a reaction, how much more should a holy God? After all, it is his law being broken. His children being abused. His word being ignored.

His holiness being insulted.

The question is not, "Couldn't God overlook sin?" The question instead is, "How in the world is forgiveness an option?" The question is not why God finds it difficult to forgive, but how he finds it possible to do so at all.[1]

From God's angle the tragedy of these men was not that they were about to die, but that they were dying with unresolved sin. They were leaving this earth hostile to God, defiant of his truth, and resistant to his call. "When people's thinking is controlled by the sinful self, they are against God" (Rom. 8:7). Sin is not an unfortunate slip or a regrettable act; it is a posture of defiance against a holy God.

Such is what heaven sees.

The figure on the center cross, however, has no such shadow of sin. "When he lived on earth, he was tempted in every way that we are, but he did not sin" (Heb. 4:15). Stainless. Selfless. Even on a sinner's cross Jesus' holiness illuminates heaven.

The first criminal reads the sign that announces Jesus as the king of the Jews. He hears Jesus pray for those who kill him. Something about the presence of the carpenter convinces him he's in the presence of a king.

The other crook has a different opinion. "Aren't you the Christ? Then save yourself and us" (Luke 23:39). You'd think a man near death would use his energy for something other than slander. Not this one. The shadow over his heart is so thick, even in pain he mocks.

Suddenly someone tells him, "You should fear God!" It's the voice of the first criminal. "We are . . . getting what we deserve for what we did. But this man has done nothing wrong" (Luke 23:41).

Finally someone is defending Jesus. Peter fled. The disciples hid. The Jews accused. Pilate washed his hands. Many could have spoken on behalf of Jesus, but none did. Until now. Kind words from the lips of a thief. He makes his request. "Jesus, remember me when you come into your kingdom" (Luke 23:42).

The Savior turns his heavy head toward the prodigal child and promises, "I tell you the truth, today you will be with me in paradise" (Luke 23:43).

To those at the foot of the cross, the dialogue was curious. But to those at the foot of the throne, the dialogue was outrageous. They couldn't imagine it. How could the thief come to paradise? How could a soul speckled by sin go to heaven? How could a sinner be saved? They were about to see.

Did an angel move, did a demon stir as they witnessed the answering of the prayer? The sins of the thief (and all us thieves!) leave him and go to Jesus. Tiny specks at first, then large flakes, and finally layers of filth. Every evil thought. Each vile deed. The thief's ravings. His cursings. His greed. His sin. All now covering Jesus Christ. What nauseates God now covers his son.

At the same instant, the purity of Jesus lifts and covers the dying thief. A sheet of radiance is wrapped around his soul. As the father robed the prodigal, so now Christ robes the thief. Not just with a clean coat but with Jesus himself! "Baptized into union with him, you have all put on Christ as a garment" (Gal. 3:27 NEB).

The One with no sin becomes sin-filled. The one sin-filled becomes sinless.

It is eternity's most bizarre exchange. Paul explained it like this: "Christ took away the curse the law put on us. He changed places with us and put himself under that curse" (Gal. 3:13).

When he sees sin, a just God must either inflict punishment or assume it. God chose the latter. On the cross "God was in Christ, making peace between the world and himself" (2 Cor. 5:19).

I know John says that Jesus was carrying his own cross as he walked up the hill, but he wasn't. He was carrying ours. The only reason he carried the cross was for us thieves and crooks. "Christ had no sin, but God made him become sin so that in Christ we could become right with God" (2 Cor. 5:21). It wasn't his death he died; it was ours. It wasn't his sin he became; it was ours.

A beautiful illustration of this came my way, even as I was writing this chapter. In between the composition of the two paragraphs above, I received a call from a friend named Kenny. He and his family had just returned from Disney World. "I saw a sight I'll never forget," he said. "I want you to know about it."

He and his family were inside Cinderella's castle. It was packed with kids and parents. Suddenly all the children rushed to one side. Had it been a boat, the castle would have tipped over. Cinderella had entered.

Cinderella. The pristine princess. Kenny said she was perfectly typecast. A gorgeous young girl with each hair in place, flawless skin, and a beaming smile. She stood waist-deep in a garden of kids, each wanting to touch and be touched.

For some reason Kenny turned and looked toward the other side of the castle. It was now vacant except for a boy maybe seven or eight years old. His age was hard to determine because of the disfigurement of his body. Dwarfed in height, face deformed, he stood watching quietly and wistfully, holding the hand of an older brother.

Don't you know what he wanted? He wanted to be with the children. He longed to be in the middle of the kids reaching for Cinderella, calling her name. But can't you feel his fear, fear of yet another rejection? Fear of being taunted again, mocked again?

Don't you wish Cinderella would go to him? Guess what? She did!

She noticed the little boy. She immediately began walking in his direction. Politely but firmly inching through the crowd of children, she finally broke free. She walked quickly across the floor, knelt at eye level with the stunned little boy, and placed a kiss on his face.

"I thought you would appreciate the story," Kenny told me. I did. It reminded me of the one you and I have been studying. The names are different, but isn't the story almost the same? Rather than a princess of Disney, we've been considering the Prince of Peace. Rather than a boy in a castle, we've looked at a thief on a cross. In both cases a gift was given. In both cases love was shared. In both cases the lovely one performed a gesture beyond words.

But Jesus did more than Cinderella. Oh, so much more.

Cinderella gave only a kiss. When she stood to leave, she took her beauty with her. The boy was still deformed. What if Cinderella had done what Jesus did? What if she'd assumed his state? What if she had somehow given him her beauty and taken on his disfigurement?

That's what Jesus did.

"He took our suffering on him and felt our pain for us. . . . He was wounded for the wrong we did; he was crushed for the evil we did. The punishment, which made us well, was given to him, and we are healed because of his wounds" (Isa. 53:4–5).

Make no mistake:

Jesus gave more than a kiss—he gave his beauty.

He paid more than a visit—he paid for our mistakes.

He took more than a minute—he took away our sin.

Then Jesus took the loaves of bread, thanked God for them, and gave them to the people who were sitting there. He did the same with the fish, giving as much as the people wanted.

John 6:11

The Bad News Preacher

The God of Stubborn Faith

I DIDN'T LIKE the preacher I sat by on the plane. I know, I know. You're supposed to like everyone, but this fellow . . .

To begin with, he took the seat next to me. I'd hoped it would stay vacant. The plane was crowded. It was a Sunday afternoon, and I was tired from Sunday-morning services. I was speaking that evening in Atlanta and had planned on taking a nap on the flight.

But this fellow had other ideas. Though he had been assigned another seat, he took the one next to me since it was closer to the front. And when he took it, he took every inch of it—and then some. Forgive me, but I get a bit territorial about armrests. This guy staked his claim on the one between us and never relinquished his position.

Knowing I couldn't sleep, I figured I'd review my thoughts for the evening lesson, so I opened my Bible.

"What ya' studying there, buddy?"

I told him, but he never heard.

"The church is lost," he declared. "Hellbound and heartsick."

Turns out he is an evangelist. He speaks in a different church every weekend. "I wake 'em up," he growled. "Christians are asleep. They don't pray. They don't love. They don't care."

With that pronouncement, he took on his preaching tone and cadence and started listing all the woes and weaknesses of the church, "Too lazy-uh, too rich-uh, too spoiled-uh, too fat-uh . . ."

The folks around were beginning to listen, and my face was beginning to redden. I shouldn't have let it bug me, but it did. I'm one of those fellows who never knows what to say at the time but then spends the next week thinking, *I wish I'd thought to say that.*

Well, I've spent the last few days thinking about it, and here is what I wish I'd said to the bad news preacher: God's faithfulness has never depended on the faithfulness of his children. He is faithful even when we aren't. When we lack courage, he doesn't. He has made a history out of using people in spite of people.

Need an example? The feeding of the five thousand. It's the only miracle, aside from those of the final week, recorded in all four Gospels. Why did all four writers think it worth repeating? Maybe they knew some preachers like the one I sat next to. Perhaps they wanted to show how God doesn't give up even when his people do.

The day begins with the news of the death of John the Baptist. It continues with the return of the disciples from a short-term missionary journey. Following the disciples are five thousand men and their families. Jesus tries to get away from the crowd by crossing the sea, only to find the crowd waiting for him on the other side. He wanted to mourn in solitude, but instead he was surrounded by people. He wanted to spend time with just the disciples, but instead he got a crowd. He wanted time to think, but instead he had people to face.[1]

He spends time teaching them, and then he turns to Philip and inquires, "Where can we buy enough bread for all these people to eat?" (John 6:5). Keep in mind that Philip has been forcing out demons and healing the sick (Mark 6:13). We'd expect him to be optimistic. A bit of faith would be appropriate. After all, he's just spent several weeks seeing the impossible happen.

But how does Philip respond? He sounds like the preacher I met on the plane. He knows the problem, but he has no clue as to the solution. "We would all have to work a month to buy enough bread for each person to have only a little piece" (John 6:7).

He can cite the stats, but he can't see how to help. He can crunch the numbers, but he can't construct the answer. And though the answer to prayer is standing next to him, he doesn't even pray.

Equally disturbing is the silence of the other disciples. Are they optimistic? Read their words, and see for yourself. "No one lives in this place and it is already very late. Send the people away so they can go to the countryside and towns around here to buy themselves something to eat" (Mark 6:35–36).

Come on, guys. How about a little faith? "You can feed them, Jesus. No challenge is too great for you. We've seen you heal the sick and raise the dead; we know you can feed the crowd."

But that's not what they said. If faith is a candle, those fellows were in the dark.

It never occurred to the disciples to turn the problem over to Jesus. Only Andrew had such a thought, but even his faith was small. "Here is a boy with five loaves of barley bread and two little fish, but that is not enough for so many people" (John 6:9).

Andrew at least comes to Jesus with an idea. But he doesn't come with much faith. In fact, one would be hard pressed to find much faith on the hill that day.

Philip was cynical.

Andrew was doubtful.

The other disciples were negative.

The preacher I met on the flight would've felt right at home with these guys. Look at them: They aren't praying, they aren't believing, they aren't even seeking a solution. If they are doing anything, they are telling Christ what to do! "Send the people away" (Mark 6:36). A bit bossy, don't you think?

Looks like the disciples are "hellbound and heartsick." Looks like they are "too lazy-uh, too rich-uh, too spoiled-uh, too fat-uh." Let me be clear. I agree with the preacher that the church is weak. When he bemoans the condition of the saints, I could sing the second verse. When he laments the health of many churches, I don't argue.

But when he proclaims that we are going to hell in a handbasket, I do! I simply think God is greater than our weakness. In fact, I think it is our weakness that reveals how great God is. He told another struggler, "When you are weak, my power is made perfect in you" (2 Cor. 12:9). The feeding of the five thousand is an ideal example. The scene answers the question, What does God do when his children are weak?

If God ever needed an excuse to give up on people, he has one here. Surely God is going to banish these followers until they learn to believe.

Is that what he does? You decide. "Then Jesus took the loaves of bread, thanked God for them, and gave them to the people who were sitting there. He did the same with the fish, giving as much as the people wanted" (John 6:11).

When the disciples didn't pray, Jesus prayed. When the disciples didn't see God, Jesus sought God. When the disciples were weak, Jesus was strong. When the disciples had no faith, Jesus had faith. He thanked God.

For what? The crowds? The pandemonium? The weariness? The faithless disciples? No, he thanked God for the basket of bread. He ignored the clouds and found the ray and thanked God for it.

Look what he does next. "Jesus divided the bread and gave it to his followers, who gave it to the people" (Matt. 14:19).

Rather than punish the disciples, he employs them. There they go, passing out the bread they didn't request, enjoying the answer to the prayer they didn't even pray. If Jesus would have acted according to the faith of his disciples, the multitudes would have gone unfed. But he didn't, and he doesn't. God is true to us even when we forget him.

God's blessings are dispensed according to the riches of his grace, not according to the depth of our faith. "If we are not faithful, he will still be faithful, because he cannot be false to himself" (2 Tim. 2:13).

Why is that important to know? So you won't get cynical. Look around you. Aren't there more mouths than bread? Aren't there more wounds than physicians? Aren't there more who need the truth than those who tell it? Aren't there more churches asleep than churches afire?

So what do we do? Throw up our hands and walk away? Tell the world we can't help them? That's what the disciples wanted to do. Should we just give up on the church? That seemed to be the approach of the preacher I met on the plane.

No, we don't give up. We look up. We trust. We believe. And our optimism is not hollow. Christ has proven worthy. He has shown that he never fails, though there is nothing but failure in us.

I'll probably never see that proclaimer of pessimism again, but maybe you will. If you do, will you give him a message for me?

God is faithful even when his children are not.

That's what makes God, God.

Jesus did many other miracles in the presence of his followers that are not written in this book. But these are written so that you may believe that Jesus is the Christ, the Son of God. Then, by believing, you may have life through his name.

John 20:30

The Final Witness

The God Who Proves His Point

JOHN DOESN'T TELL us everything Jesus did. But he tells us those acts that will lead us to faith. John selects seven miracles. He begins softly with the quiet miracle of water to wine and then crescendos to the public resurrection of Lazarus. Seven miracles are offered, and seven witnesses are examined, each one building on the testimony of the previous.

Let's see if we can feel their full impact.

Pretend you are in a courtroom, a nearly empty courtroom. Present are four people: a judge, a lawyer, an orphan, and a would-be guardian. The judge is God, Jesus is the one who seeks to be the guardian, and you are the orphan. You have no name, no inheritance, no home. The lawyer is proposing that you be placed in Jesus' care.

Who is the lawyer? A Galilean fisherman by the name of John.

He has presented the court with six witnesses. It is time for the seventh. But before calling him to the stand, the lawyer reviews the case. "We started this case with the wedding in Cana." He paces as he speaks, measuring each word. "They had no wine, none at all. But when Jesus spoke, water became wine. The best wine. Delicious wine. You heard the testimony of the wedding attendants. They saw it happen."

He pauses, then moves on. "Then we heard the words of the foreign official. His son was nearly dead."

You nod. You remember the man's testimony. Articulate, he had spoken of how he had called every doctor and tried every treatment, but nothing had helped his son. Just when he was about to give up hope, someone told him about a healer in Galilee.

Through his thickened accent the dignitary had explained, "I had no other choice. I went to him out of desperation. Look! Look what the teacher did for my son." The boy had stood, and you had stared. It was hard to believe such a healthy youngster had ever been near death.

You listen intently as John continues, "And, your honor, don't forget the crippled man near the pool. For thirty-eight years he had not walked. But then Jesus came and, well, the court saw him. Remember? We saw him walk into this room. We heard his story.

"And, as if that was not enough, we also heard the testimony of the boy with the lunch. He was part of a crowd of thousands who had followed Jesus in order to hear him teach and to see him heal. Just when the little boy was about to open his lunch basket to eat, he was asked to bring it to Jesus. One minute it held a lunch; the next it held a feast."

John pauses again, letting the silence of the courtroom speak. No one can deny these testimonies. The judge listens. The lawyer listens. And you, the orphan, say nothing.

"Then there was the storm. Peter described it to us. The boat bouncing on the waves. Thunder. Lightning. Storms like that can kill. I know. I used to make a living on a boat! Peter's testimony about what happened was true. I was there. The Master walked on the water. And the moment he stepped into the boat, we were safe."

John pauses again. Sunlight squared by a window makes a box on the floor. John steps into the box. "Then, yesterday, you met a man who had never seen light. His world was dark. Black. He was blind. Blind from birth."

John pauses and dramatically states what the man born blind had said: "Jesus healed my eyes."

Six testimonies have been given. Six miracles have been verified. John gestures toward the table where sit the articles of evidence: The water jugs that held the wine. The signed affidavit of the doctor who'd treated the sick son. The cot of the cripple, the basket of the boy. Peter had brought a broken oar to show the strength of the storm. And the blind man had left his cup and cane. He didn't need to beg anymore.

"And now," John says, turning to the judge, "we have one final witness to call and one more piece of evidence to submit."

He goes to his table and returns with a white linen sheet. You lean forward, unsure of what he is holding. "This is a burial shroud," he explains. Placing the clothing on the table he requests, "Your honor permitting, I call our final witness to the chair, Lazarus of Bethany."

Heavy courtroom doors open, and a tall man enters. He strides down the aisle and pauses before Jesus long enough to place a hand on his shoulder and say, "Thank you." You can hear the tenderness in his voice. Lazarus then turns and takes his seat in the witness chair.

"State your name for the court."

"Lazarus."

"Have you heard of a man called Jesus of Nazareth?"

"Who hasn't?"

"How do you know him?"

"He is my friend. We, my sisters and I, have a house in Bethany. When he comes to Jerusalem, he often stays with us. My sisters, Mary and Martha, have become believers in him as well."

"Believers?"

"Believers that he is the Messiah. The Son of God."

"Why do you believe that?"

Lazarus smiles. "How could I not believe? I was dead. I had been dead for four days. I was in the tomb. I was prayed for and buried. I was dead. But Jesus called me out of the grave."

"Tell us what happened."

"Well, I've always been sickly. That's why I've stayed with my sisters, you know. They care for me. My heart never has been the strongest, so I have to be careful. Martha, the oldest sister, she's, well, she's like a mother to me. It was Martha who called Jesus when my heart failed."

"Is that when you died?"

"No, but almost. I lingered for a few days. But I knew I was near the edge. The doctors would just come in and shake their heads and walk out. I had one sandal in the grave."

"Is that when Jesus came?"

"No, we kept hoping he would. Martha would sit by the bed at night, and she would whisper over and over and over, 'Be strong, Lazarus. Jesus will be here any minute.' We just knew he would come. I mean, he had healed all those strangers; surely he would heal me. I was his friend."

"What delayed him?"

"For the longest time we didn't know. I thought he might be in prison or something. I kept waiting and waiting. Every day I got weaker. My vision faded, and I couldn't see. I drifted in and out. Every time someone entered my room, I thought it might be him. But it never was. He never came."

"Were you angry?"

"More confused than angry. I just didn't understand."

"Then what happened?"

"Well, I woke up one night. My chest was so tight I could hardly breathe. I must have sat up because Martha and Mary came to my bed. They took my hand. I heard them calling my name, but then I began to fall. It was like a dream, I was falling, spinning wildly in midair. Their voices grew fainter and fainter and then nothing. The spinning stopped, the falling stopped. And the hurting stopped. I was at peace."

"At peace?"

"Like I was asleep. Resting. Tranquil. I was dead."

"Then what happened?"

"Well, Martha can tell the details. The funeral was planned. The family came. Friends traveled from Jerusalem. They buried me."

"Did Jesus come to the funeral?"

"No."

"He still wasn't there?"

"No, when he heard I was buried, he waited an extra four days."

"Why?"

Lazarus stopped and looked at Jesus. "To make his point."

John smiled knowingly.

"What happened next?"

"I heard his voice."

"Whose voice?"

"The voice of Jesus."

"But I thought you were dead."

"I was."

"I, uh, thought you were in a grave."

"I was."

"How does a dead man in a grave hear the voice of a man?"

"He doesn't. The dead hear only the voice of God. I heard the voice of God."

"What did he say?"

"He didn't say it; he shouted it."

"What did he shout?"

"'Lazarus, come out!'"

"And you heard him?"

"As if he were in the tomb with me. My eyes opened; my fingers moved. I lifted my head. I was alive again. I heard the stone being rolled away. The light poured in. It took a minute for my eyes to adjust."

"What did you see?"

"A circle of faces looking in at me."

"Then what did you do?"

"I stood up. Jesus gave me his hand and pulled me out. He told the people to get me some real clothes, and they did."

"So you died, were in the tomb four days, then Jesus called you back to life? Were there any witnesses to this?"

Lazarus chuckles. "Only a hundred or so."

"That's all, Lazarus, thank you. You may step down."

John returns to the judge. "You have heard the testimonies. I now leave the decision in your hands." With that he returns to the table and takes his seat. The guardian stands. He doesn't identify himself. He doesn't need to. All recognize him. He is Jesus Christ.

Jesus' voice fills the courtroom. "I represent an orphan who is the sum of all you have seen. Like the party that had no wine, this one has no cause for celebration. Like the dignitary's son, this child is spiritually ill. Like the cripple and the beggar, he can't walk and is blind. He is starving, but earth has no food to fill him. He faces storms as severe as the one on Galilee, but earth has no compass to guide him. And most of all, he is dead. Just like Lazarus. Dead. Spiritually dead."

"I will do for him what I did for them. I'll give him joy, strength, healing, sight, safety, nourishment, new life. All are his. If you will permit."

The judge speaks his answer. "You are my Son, whom I love, and I am very pleased with you" (Luke 3:22). God looks at you. "I will permit it," he says, "on one condition. That the orphan request it."

John has presented the witnesses.

The witnesses have told their stories.

The Master has offered to do for you what he did for them. He will bring wine to your table, sight to your eyes, strength for your step and, most of all, power over your grave. He will do for you what he did for them.

The Judge has given his blessing. The rest is up to you.

Now the choice is yours.

Our Choice

On one side stands the crowd.
    Jeering.
        Baiting.
        Demanding.

On the other stands a peasant.
    Swollen lips.
        Lumpy eye.
        Lofty promise.

One promises acceptance,
    the other a cross.
One offers flesh and flash,
    the other offers faith.

The crowd challenges, "Follow us and fit in."
    Jesus promises, "Follow me and stand out."

They promise to please.
    God promises to save.

A basin of water?
    Or the blood of the Savior?

God looks at you and asks . . .
    Which will be your choice?

I tell you the truth, unless one is born again, he cannot be in God's kingdom.

John 3:3

Inside Out

Born Once or Born Twice?

Two sons of the king brought their father a question. "Is a gentleman born or made?"

"What do you think? he replied.

"I think a gentleman is born a gentleman," replied one son.

"I disagree," replied the other. "A man becomes a gentleman by training and discipline."

The king looked at his sons and issued a challenge. "Prove your case by presenting me an example. I give each of you a week to return with proof of your opinions."

And so the two sons departed in different directions. The son who believed a gentleman was made, not born, found his proof in a tavern. He'd ordered a cup of tea and was amazed when he saw that the waiter was a cat. This cat had been trained to stand on his hind legs and carry the tray in his forepaws. He wore a tiny uniform and hat and was proof that a creature could overcome his nature with training and discipline.

The first son had his example. If a cat can be changed, couldn't a man? So the prince purchased the animal and took him to the court.

The other son was not so fortunate. He'd searched the kingdom but was unable to find any support for his theory. He returned home empty-handed. What's worse, word had leaked about his brother's discovery. News of the walking cat made him doubt his convictions. But then, just hours before the two were to appear before the king, he saw something in a store window that made him smile.

He made the purchase but told no one.

The two sons entered the court of the king, each one carrying a box. The first son announced that he could prove that a man could overcome any obstacle and become a gentleman. As the king watched, the son presented the cat, dressed in miniature court dress, who gave the king a tray of chocolates.

The king was stunned, his son was proud, and the court broke into applause. What excellent proof! Who could deny the evidence of the walking cat? Everyone pitied the second son. But he was not discouraged. With a bow to the king, he opened the box he had brought, releasing several mice into the court. Instantly the cat scampered after the mice.[1]

The cat's true nature had been revealed, and the point had been made. A walking cat is still a cat. You can change his clothes. You can teach him tricks. You can give him a hat and train him to walk. And for a while he will appear to be changed. But present him with the one thing he can't resist, and you'll be faced with an undeniable truth—a walking cat is still a cat.

The same is true with people. We can change our clothes. We can change our habits. We can change our vocabulary, our reading level, even our attitude. But according to the Bible, there is one thing we cannot change—our sinful state.

Society would agree with the first son. It says change the outside and the inside will follow. Give a person education, training, the right habits, and the right disciplines, and the person will be changed. Oh, we try. Boy, do we try. We buy clothes. We seek degrees, awards, achievements.

We tell it to our kids. *Make something of your life.*

We tell it to our employees. *Act yourself into a better way of feeling.*

We tell it to the discouraged. *Try, try again.*

We even tell it to our church members. *Come to church, and you'll have a better attitude.*

But peel away the layers, take away the costumes, remove the makeup, and underneath you see our true nature—a selfish, prideful, sinful heart. Just bring out the mice and see what we do.

No one describes it better than Paul. Listen to his confession:

> I realize that I don't have what it takes. I can will it, but I can't do it. I decide to do good, but I don't really do it; I decide not to do bad, but then I do it anyway. My decisions, such as they are, don't result in actions. Something has gone wrong deep within me and gets the better of me every time.
>
> It happens so regularly that it's predictable. The moment I decide to do good, sin is there to trip me up. I truly delight in God's commands, but it's pretty obvious that not all of me joins in that delight. Parts of me covertly rebel, and just when I least expect it, they take charge.
>
> I've tried everything and nothing helps. I'm at the end of my rope. Is there no one who can do anything for me? Isn't that the real question? (Rom. 7:18–24, TM)

Paul is saying that no matter what I do, how hard I try, how much I strive, I still sin against God. Put clothes on me, teach me to walk on my hind legs, take me into the presence of the king himself, but let a few mice cross my trail and *BOOM*! The real me comes out.

I lose my temper,

    I forget my purpose,

        I demand my way,

            I lie,

                I lust,

                    I turn,

                        I fall . . .

The animal within takes over.

Please remember who wrote those words. The apostle Paul! Paul, the missionary. Paul, the zealot. Paul, the martyr. Paul, the Bible writer.

Paul, the sinner.

The same Paul who asked the question, "Who will save me from this body that brings me death?" and the Paul who answered the dilemma by proclaiming, "I thank God for saving me through Jesus Christ our Lord" (Rom. 7:25).

Changing the clothes doesn't change the man. Outward discipline doesn't alter what is within. New habits don't make a new soul. That's not to say that outward change is not good. That is to say that outward change is not enough. If one would see the kingdom, he must be born again.

That phrase, *born again*, belongs to Jesus. He first used it when he was talking to Nicodemus. Nicodemus was a good man. A very good man. He was a Pharisee, a religious ruler, a member of the Sanhedrin, one of the decision makers in Jerusalem. No doubt he had been taught and had taught that if you change the outside, you change the inside. He, like Paul, revered the law. He, like Paul, wanted to do right.

He thought the right training could make a waiter out of a cat.

But Jesus told him, "I tell you the truth, unless one is born again, he cannot be in God's kingdom" (John 3:3). Nicodemus's response is sincere. He didn't ask *Why*? He asked *How*? Perhaps you are asking the same question. How is a person born again?

To get an idea, think back to your own birth. Put the VCR of your days in reverse, and pause at your first moments. Look at yourself. Brand-new. New hands. New eyes. New mouth. No pre-owned parts. All original material.

Now tell me, who gave you these parts? Who gave you eyes so you could see? Who gave you hands so you could work? Who gave you feet that you could walk? Did you make your own eyes? Your own hands? Your own feet?

No, you made nothing; God made everything. He was the one who made everything new the first time, and he is the one who makes everything new the second. The Creator creates again! "If anyone belongs to Christ, there is a new creation. The old things have gone; everything is made new!" (2 Cor. 5:17)

Here is (dare I say it?) the greatest miracle of God. It is astounding when God heals the body. It is extraordinary when God hears the prayer. It is incredible when God provides the new job, the new car, the new child. But none of these compares to when God creates new life.

At our new birth God remakes our souls and gives us what we need, again. New eyes so we can see by faith. A new mind so we can have the mind of Christ. New strength so we won't grow tired. A new vision so we won't lose heart. A new voice for praise and new hands for service. And most of all, a new heart. A heart that has been cleansed by Christ.

And, oh, how we need it. We have soiled what he gave us the first time. We have used our eyes to see impurity, our hands to give pain, our feet to walk the wrong path, our minds to think evil thoughts. All of us need to be made new again.

The first birth was for earthly life; the second one is for eternal life. The first time we received a physical heart; the second time we receive a spiritual heart. The first birth enabled us to have life on earth. The second birth enables us to have life eternal.

But the analogy contains another truth. May I ask another question about your birth? How active were you in the process? (Don't look at me like that. Of course I'm being serious.) How active were you? Did you place your hands against the top of the womb and shove yourself out? Were you in radio communication with your mother, telling her when to push? Did the doctor ask you to measure the contractions and report on conditions inside the womb?

Hardly. You were passive. You were not born because of what you did. Someone else did all the work. Someone else felt all the pain. Your mom did the pushing and the struggling. Your birth was due to someone else's effort.

The same is true for our spiritual birth. It is through God's pain that we are born. It's not our struggle, but God's. It's not our blood shed, but his.

Jesus illustrates this by reminding Nicodemus of Moses lifting up the serpent in the wilderness. "Just as Moses lifted up the snake in the desert, so the Son of Man must be lifted up" (John 3:14). Israel had been complaining against God, and so God sent snakes that bit the people. Some died, and others were dying. The people confessed that they had sinned and cried to Moses for relief. Moses turned to God, and the Father told him to make a brass snake and fix it on a pole and tell the bitten people to look on it in faith and they would be healed.

Just as the serpent was lifted up . . . so the Christ was lifted up. Just as the serpent was fixed to a pole . . . so on the cross Christ nailed the power of the serpent of Eden to a pole. And just as the snake was a curse . . . so Christ became a curse for us (Gal. 3:13). And just as the people were healed when they looked on the serpent, so we are healed when we look to the cross.

That's all the people were commanded to do.

The poisoned people weren't told to take medicine or to extract the poison by suction. They weren't told to engage in good works to make an offering. They weren't told to examine their wounds, argue their plight, or pray to the serpent. Nor were they told to look at Moses. They were told simply, oh, how simply, to look to Christ.

Sin began when Eve looked at the tree (see Gen. 3:6). Salvation comes when we look to Christ. Astonishing simplicity. Summarized in the great promise of John 3:16: "God loved the world so much that he gave his one and only Son so that whoever believes in him may not be lost, but have eternal life."

God, the Lover. God, the Giver. God, the Savior. And man, the believer. And for those who believe, he has promised a new birth.

But despite the simplicity, there are still those who don't believe. They don't trust the promise. They can't imagine how God would know their name, much less forgive their sins. It's almost too good to be true.

If only they would try. If only they would test it. But God is as polite as he is passionate. He never forces his way in. The choice is theirs.

And for those who do come, he has promised a new birth.

Does that mean you'll never chase mice again? Does that mean the old nature will never rear its ugly head? Does that mean you will instantly be able to resist any temptation?

Go to the delivery room to answer that question. Look at the newborn baby. What can he do? Can he walk? Can he feed himself? Can he sing or read or speak? No, not yet. But someday he will.

It takes time to grow. But is the parent in the delivery room ashamed of the baby? Is the mom embarrassed that the infant can't spell . . . that the baby can't walk . . . that the newborn can't give a speech?

Of course not. The parents aren't ashamed; they are proud. They know that growth will come with time. So does God. "God is being patient with you. He does not want anyone to be lost, but he wants all people to change their hearts and lives" (2 Pet. 3:9).

God is often more patient with us than we are with ourselves. We assume that if we fall, we aren't born again. If we stumble, then we aren't truly converted. If we have the old desires, then we must not be a new creation.

If you are anxious about this, please remember, "God began doing a good work in you, and I am sure he will continue it until it is finished when Jesus Christ comes again" (Phil. 1:6).

In many ways your new birth is like your first: In your new birth God provides what you need; someone else feels the pain, and someone else does the work. And just as parents are patient with their newborn, so God is patient with you. But there is one difference. The first time you had no choice about being born; this time you do. The power is God's. The effort is God's. The pain is God's. But the choice is yours.

I am a man who has told you the truth which I heard from God. . . . But because I speak the truth, you don't believe me.

John 8:40, 45

The Yay-Yuck Man

The Crowds or the Christ

BOB LOVED TO make people happy.

Bob lived to make people happy.

If people weren't happy, Bob wasn't happy. So every day Bob set out to make people happy. Not an easy task, for what makes some people happy makes other people angry.

Bob lived in a land where everyone wore coats. The people never removed their coats. Bob never asked *Why?* He only asked *Which?* "Which coat should I wear?"

Bob's mother loved blue. So to please her he wore a blue coat. When she would see him wearing blue she would say, "Yay, Bob! I love it when you wear blue." So he wore the blue coat all the time. And since he never left his house and since he saw no one but his mother, he was happy, for she was happy and she said "Yay, Bob" over and over.

Bob grew up and got a job. The first day of his first job he got up early and put on his best blue coat and walked down the street.

The crowds on the street, however, didn't like blue. They liked green. Everyone on the street wore green. As he walked past, everyone looked at his blue coat and said, "Yuck!"

Yuck! was a hard word for Bob to hear. He felt guilty that he had caused a "yuck" to come out of a person's mouth. He loved to hear "yay!" He hated to hear "yuck!"

When the people saw his blue coat and said "yuck," Bob dashed into a clothing store and bought a green coat. He put it on over his blue coat and walked back out in the street. "Yay!" the people shouted as he walked past. He felt better because he had made them feel better.

When he arrived at his workplace, he walked into his boss's office wearing a green coat. "Yuck!" said his boss.

"Oh, I'm sorry," said Bob, quickly removing the green coat and revealing the blue. "You must be like my mother."

"Double yuck!" responded the boss. He got up from his chair, walked to the closet, and produced a yellow coat. "We like yellow here," he instructed.

"Whatever you say, sir," Bob answered, relieved to know he wouldn't have to hear his boss say "yuck" anymore. He put the yellow coat over the green coat, which was over the blue coat. And so he went to work.

When it was time for him to go home, he replaced the yellow coat with the green and walked through the streets. Just before he got to his house, he put the blue coat over the green and yellow coats and went inside.

Bob learned that life with three coats was hard. His movements were stiff, and he was always hot. There were also times when the cuff of one coat would peek out and someone would notice, but before the person could say "yuck" Bob would tuck it away.

One day he forgot to change his coat before he went home, and when his mother saw green she turned purple with disgust and started to say, "Yuck." But before she could, Bob ran and put his hand on her mouth and held the word in while he traded coats and then removed his hand so she said, "Yay!"

It was at this moment that Bob realized he had a special gift. He could change his colors with ease. With a little practice, he was able to shed one coat and replace it with another in a matter of seconds.

Even Bob didn't understand his versatility, but he was pleased with it. For now he could be any color anytime and please every person.

His skill at changing coats quickly elevated him to high positions. Everyone liked him because everyone thought he was just like them. With time he was elected mayor over the entire city.

His acceptance speech was brilliant. Those who loved green thought he was wearing green. Those who loved yellow thought he was wearing yellow, and his mother just knew he was wearing blue. Only he knew that he was constantly changing from one to the other.

It wasn't easy, but it was worth it, because at the end everyone said, "Yay!"

Bob's multicolored life continued until one day some yellow-coated people stormed into his office. "We have found a criminal who needs to be executed," they announced, shoving a man toward Bob's desk. Bob was shocked at what he saw. The man wasn't wearing a coat at all, just a T-shirt.

"Leave him with me," Bob instructed, and the yellow coats left.

"Where is your coat?" asked the mayor.

"I don't wear one."

"You don't have one?"

"I don't want one."

"You don't want a coat? But everyone wears a coat. It, it, it's the way things are here."

"I'm not from here."

"What coat do they wear where you are from?"

"No coat."

"None?"

"None."

Bob looked at the man with amazement. "But what if people don't approve?"

"It's not their approval I seek."

Bob had never heard such words. He didn't know what to say. He'd never met a person without a coat. The man with no coat spoke again.

"I am here to show people they don't have to please people. I am here to tell the truth."

If Bob had ever heard of the word *truth*, he'd long since rejected it. "What is truth?" he asked.

But before the man could answer, people outside the mayor's office began to scream, "Kill him! Kill him!"

A mob had gathered outside the window. Bob went to it and saw the crowd was wearing green. Putting on his green coat, he said, "There is nothing wrong with this man."

"Yuck!" they shouted. Bob fell back at the sound.

By then the yellow coats were back in his office. Seeing them, Bob changed his colors and pleaded, "The man is innocent."

"Yuck!" they proclaimed. Bob covered his ears at the word.

He looked at the man and pleaded, "Who are you?"

The man answered simply, "Who are you?"

Bob did not know. But suddenly he wanted to. Just then his mother, who'd heard of the crisis, entered the office. Without realizing it, Bob changed to blue. "He is not one of us," she said.

"But, but, . . ."

"Kill him!"

A torrent of voices came from all directions. Bob again covered his ears and looked at the man with no coat. The man was silent. Bob was tormented. "I can't please them and set you free!" he shouted over their screams.

The man with no coat was silent.

"I can't please you and them!"

Still the man was silent.

"Speak to me!" Bob demanded.

The man with no coat spoke one word. "Choose."

"I can't!" Bob declared. He threw up his hands and screamed, "Take him, I wash my hands of the choice."

But even Bob knew in making no choice he had made one. The man was led away, and Bob was left alone. Alone with his coats.

When all the wine was gone, Jesus' mother said to him, "They have no more wine."

John 2:3

Calamities of the Common Scale

Worry or Trust?

YOU'RE AT YOUR best friend's wedding reception. The two of you have talked about this day since you were kids, and now it's here. The ceremony was great; the wedding was beautiful. The minister was flawless, and the vows were honest. What a day!

"I'll take care of the reception," you'd volunteered. You planned the best party possible. You hired the band, rented the hall, catered the meal, decorated the room, and asked your Aunt Bertha to bake the cake.

Now the band is playing and the guests are milling, but Aunt Bertha is nowhere to be seen. Everything is here but the cake. You sneak over to the pay phone and dial her number. She's been taking a nap. She thought the wedding was next week.

Oh boy! Now what do you do? Talk about a problem! Everything is here but the cake . . .

Sound familiar?

It might. It's exactly the dilemma Jesus' mother, Mary, was facing. The wedding was moving. The guests were celebrating . . . but the wine was gone. Back then, wine was to a wedding what cake is to a wedding today. Can you imagine a wedding without cake? They couldn't imagine a wedding without wine. To offer wine was to show respect to your guests. Not to offer wine at a wedding was an insult.

What Mary faced was a social problem. A foul-up. A snafu. A calamity on the common scale. No need to call 911, but no way to sweep the embarrassment under the rug, either.

When you think about it, most of the problems we face are of the same caliber. Seldom do we have to deal with dilemmas of national scale or world conflict. Seldom do our crises rock the Richter scale. Usually the waves we ride are made by pebbles, not boulders. We're late for a meeting. We leave something at the office. A coworker forgets a report. Mail gets lost. Traffic gets snarled. The waves rocking our lives are not life threatening yet. But they can be. A poor response to a simple problem can light a fuse. What begins as a snowflake can snowball into an avalanche unless proper care is taken.

For that reason you might want to note how Mary reacted. Her solution poses a practical plan for untangling life's knots. "They have no more wine," she told Jesus (John 2:3). That's it. That's all she said. She didn't go ballistic. She simply assessed the problem and gave it to Christ.

"A problem well stated is a problem half solved," John Dewey said. Mary would have liked that, for that's what she did. She defined the problem.

She could have exploded: "Why didn't you plan better? There's not enough wine! Whose fault is this anyway? You guys never do anything right. If anything is to be done right around here I have to do it myself!"

Or she could have imploded: "This is my fault. I failed. I'm to blame. I deserve it. If only I'd majored in culinary art. I'm a failure in life. Go ahead; do the world a favor. Tie me up and march me to the gallows. I deserve it."

It's so easy to focus on everything but the solution. Mary didn't do that. She simply looked at the knot, assessed it, and took it to the right person. "I've got one here I can't untie, Jesus."

"When all the wine was gone Jesus' mother said to him, 'They have no more wine'" (John 2:3).

Please note, she took the problem to Jesus before she took it to anyone else. A friend told me about a tense deacons' meeting he attended. Apparently there was more agitation than agreement, and after a lengthy discussion, someone suggested, "Why don't we pray about it?" to which another questioned, "Has it come to that?"

What causes us to think of prayer as the last option rather than the first? I can think of two reasons: feelings of independence and feelings of insignificance.

Sometimes we're independent. We begin to think we are big enough to solve our own problems.

At our house we have had a banner year. Our third daughter has learned how to swim. That means that three can walk. Three can swim. And two out of the three have the training wheels off their bikes. With each achievement they have delightedly pointed out, "Look, Dad, I can do it on my own." Denalyn and I have applauded and celebrated each accomplishment our daughters have made. Their maturity and mobility is good and necessary, but I hope they never get to the point where they are too grown up to call their daddy.

God feels the same way about us.

Other times we don't feel independent; we feel insignificant. We think, "Sure, Mary can take her problems to Jesus. She's his mother. He doesn't want to hear my problems. Besides, he's got famine and the Mafia to deal with. I don't want to trouble him with my messes."

If that is your thought, may I share with you a favorite verse of mine? (Of course I can, I'm writing the book!) I like it so much I wrote it on the first page of my Bible.

"Because he delights in me, he saved me" (Ps. 18:19).

And you thought he saved you because of your decency. You thought he saved you because of your good works or good attitude or good looks. Sorry. If that were the case, your salvation would be lost when your voice went south or your works got weak. There are many reasons God saves you: to bring glory to himself, to appease his justice, to demonstrate his sovereignty. But one of the sweetest reasons God saved you is because he is fond of you. He likes having you around. He thinks you are the best thing to come down the pike in quite awhile. "As a man rejoices over his new wife, so your God will rejoice over you" (Isa. 62:5).

If God had a refrigerator, your picture would be on it. If he had a wallet, your photo would be in it. He sends you flowers every spring and a sunrise every morning. Whenever you want to talk, he'll listen. He can live anywhere in the universe, and he chose your heart. And the Christmas gift he sent you in Bethlehem? Face it, friend. He's crazy about you.

The last thing you should worry about is being a nuisance to God. All you need to concentrate on is doing what he tells you to do. Note the sequence of events in the next verse: "Jesus said to the servants, 'Fill the jars with water.' So they filled the jars to the top. Then he said to them, 'Now take some out and give it to the master of the feast.' So they took the water to the master. When he tasted it, the water had become wine" (John 2:7–9).

Did you see the sequence? First the jars were filled with water. Then Jesus instructed the servants to take the water (not the wine) to the master.

Now, if I'm a servant, I don't want to do that. How is that going to solve the problem? And what is the master going to say when I give him a cup of water? But these servants either had enough naivete or trust to do what Jesus said, and so the problem was solved. Note, the water became wine after they had obeyed, not before.

What if the servants had refused? What if they had said, "No way"? Or, to bring the point closer to home, what if *you* refuse? What if you identify the problem, take it to Jesus, and then refuse to do what he says?

That's possible. After all, God is asking you to take some pretty gutsy steps. Money is tight, but he still asks you to give. You've been offended, but he asks you to forgive your offender. Someone else blew the assignment, but he still asks you to be patient. You can't see God's face, but he still asks you to pray.

Not commands for the faint of faith. But then again, he wouldn't ask you to do it if he thought you couldn't. So go ahead. Next time you face a common calamity, follow the example of Mary at the wineless wedding:

Identify the problem. (You'll half-solve it.)

Present it to Jesus. (He's happy to help.)

Do what he says. (No matter how crazy.)

And buy your Aunt Bertha a new calendar.

They had a dinner for Jesus. Martha served the food, and Lazarus was one of the people eating with Jesus. Mary brought in a pint of very expensive perfume made from pure nard. She poured the perfume on his feet, and then she wiped his feet with her hair. And the sweet smell from the perfume filled the whole house.

John 12:2–3

Your Place in God's Band

At Work or at Odds?

TWO OF MY teenage years were spent carrying a tuba in my high school marching band. My mom wanted me to learn to read music, and the choir was full while the band was a tuba-tooter short, so I signed up. Not necessarily what you would describe as a call from God, but it wasn't a wasted experience either.

I had a date with a twirler.

I learned to paint white shoe polish on school buses.

I learned that when you don't know your music, you need to put your lips to the horn and pretend you do rather than play and remove all doubt.

And I learned some facts about harmony that I'll pass on to you.

I marched next to the bass-drum player. What a great sound. *Boom. Boom. Boom.* Deep, cavernous, thundering. At the right measure in the right music, there is nothing better than the sound of a bass drum. *Boom. Boom. Boom.*

And at the end of my flank marched the flute section. Oh, how their music soared. Whispering, lifting, rising into the clouds.

Ahead of me, at the front of my line, was our first-chair trumpet. A band member through and through. While some guys shot hoops and others drove hot rods, he played the trumpet. And it showed.

Put him on the fifty yard line and let him blow. He could raise the spirit. He could raise the flag. He could have raised the roof on the stadium if we'd had one.

Flute and trumpets sound very different. (See? I told you I learned a lot in band.) The flute whispers. The trumpet shouts. The flute comforts. The trumpet bugles. There's nothing like a trumpet—in limited dosages. A person can only be blasted at for so long. After a while you need to hear something softer. Something sweeter. You need to hear a little flute. But even the sound of the flute can go flat if there is no rhythm or cadence. That's why you also need the drum.

But who wants the drum all by itself? Ever seen a band made up of bass drums? Would you attend a concert of a hundred drums? Probably not. But what band would want to be without a bass drum or flute or trumpet?

The soft flute
    needs
        the brash trumpet
          needs
            the steady drum
            needs
              the soft flute
              needs
                the brash trumpet.

Get the idea? The operative word is *need*. They need each other. By themselves they make music. But together, they make magic.

Now, what I saw two decades ago in the band, I see today in the church. We need each other. Not all of us play the same instrument. Some believers are lofty, and others are solid. Some keep the pace while others lead the band. Not all of us make the same sound. Some are soft, and others are loud. And not all of us have the same ability. Some need to be on the fifty yard line raising the flag. Others need to be in the background playing backup. But each of us has a place.

Some play the drums (like Martha).

Some play the flute (like Mary).

And others sound the trumpet (like Lazarus).

Mary, Martha, and Lazarus were like family to Jesus. After the Lord raised Lazarus from the dead, they decided to give a dinner for Jesus. They decided to honor him by having a party on his behalf (see John 12:2).

They didn't argue over the best seat. They didn't resent each other's abilities. They didn't try to outdo each other. All three worked together with one purpose. But each one fulfilled that purpose in his or her unique manner. Martha served; she always kept everyone in step. Mary worshiped; she anointed her Lord with an extravagant gift, and its aroma filled the air. Lazarus had a story to tell, and he was ready to tell it.

Three people, each one with a different skill, a different ability. But each one of equal value. Think about it. Could their family have done without one of the three?

Could we do without one of the three today?

Every church needs a Martha. Change that. Every church needs a hundred Marthas. Sleeves rolled and ready, they keep the pace for the church. Because of Marthas, the church budget gets balanced, the church babies get bounced, and the church building gets built. You don't appreciate Marthas until a Martha is missing, and then all the Marys and Lazaruses are scrambling around looking for the keys and the thermostats and the overhead projectors.

Marthas are the Energizer bunnies of the church. They keep going and going and going. They store strength like a camel stores water. Since they don't seek the spotlight, they don't live off the applause. That's not to say they don't need it. They just aren't addicted to it.

Marthas have a mission. In fact, if Marthas have a weakness, it is their tendency to elevate the mission over the Master. Remember when Martha did that? A younger Martha invites a younger Jesus to come for dinner. Jesus accepts and brings his disciples.

The scene Luke describes has Mary seated and Martha fuming. Martha is angry because Mary is, horror of horrors, sitting at the feet of Jesus. How impractical! How irrelevant! How unnecessary! I mean, who has time to sit and listen when there is bread to be baked, tables to be set, and souls to be saved? So Martha complained, "Lord, don't you care that my sister has left me alone to do all the work? Tell her to help me" (Luke 10:40).

My, my! Aren't we testy? All of a sudden Martha has gone from serving Jesus to making demands of Jesus. The room falls silent. The disciples duck their eyes. Mary flushes red. And Jesus speaks. He speaks not only to Martha of Bethany, but to all Marthas who tend to think that a bass drum is the only instrument in the band.

"Martha, Martha, you are worried and upset about many things. Only one thing is important. Mary has chosen the better thing, and it will never be taken away from her" (Luke 10:41–42).

Apparently Martha got the point, for later we find her serving again.

"Here a dinner was given in Jesus' honor. Martha served, while Lazarus was among those reclining at the table with him. Then Mary took about a pint of pure nard, an expensive perfume; she poured it on Jesus' feet and wiped his feet with her hair. And the house was filled with the fragrance of the perfume" (John 12:2–3 NIV).

Is Mary in the kitchen? No, she is playing her flute for Jesus. She is worshiping, for that is what she loves to do. But this time Martha doesn't object. She has learned that there is a place for praise and worship, and that is what Mary is doing. And what is Mary's part in the dinner? She brings a pint of very expensive perfume and pours it on Jesus' feet, then wipes his feet with her hair. The smell of the perfume fills the house, just like the sound of praise can fill a church.

An earlier Martha would have objected. Such an act was too lavish, too extravagant, too generous. But this mature Martha has learned that just as there is a place in the kingdom of God for sacrificial service, there is also a place for extravagant praise.

Marys are gifted with praise. They don't just sing; they worship. They don't simply attend church; they go to offer praise. They don't just talk about Christ; they radiate Christ.

Marys have one foot in heaven and the other on a cloud. It's not easy for them to come to earth, but sometimes they need to. Sometimes they need to be reminded that there are bills to be paid and classes to be taught. But don't remind them too harshly. Flutes are fragile. Marys are precious souls with tender hearts. If they have found a place at the foot of Jesus, don't ask them to leave. Much better to ask them to pray for you.

That's what I do. When I find a Mary (or a Michael), I'm quick to ask, "How do I get on your prayer list?"

Every church desperately needs some Marys.

We need them to pray for our children.

We need them to put passion in our worship.

We need them to write songs of praise and sing songs of glory.

We need them to kneel and weep and lift their hands and pray.

We need them because we tend to forget how much God loves worship. Marys don't forget. They know that God wants to be known as a father. They know that a father likes nothing more than to have his children sit as his feet and spend time with him.

Marys are good at that.

They, too, must be careful. They must meditate often on Luke 6:46. "Why do you call me 'Lord, Lord,' but do not do what I say?"

Marys need to remember that service is worship.

Marthas need to remember that worship is service.

And Lazarus? He needs to remember that not everyone can play the trumpet.

You see, as far as we know, Lazarus did nothing at the dinner. He saved his actions for outside the house. Read carefully John 12:9:

"A large crowd of Jews heard that Jesus was in Bethany. So they went there to see not only Jesus, but Lazarus, whom Jesus raised from the dead. So the leading priests made plans to kill Lazarus, too. Because of Lazarus many Jews were leaving them and believing in Jesus."

Wow! Because of Lazarus many Jews were "believing in Jesus."

Lazarus has been given a trumpet. He has a testimony to give—and what a testimony he has!

"I was always a good fellow," he would say. "I paid my bills. I loved my sisters. I even enjoyed being around Jesus. But I wasn't one of the followers. I didn't get as close as Peter and James and those guys. I kept my distance. Nothing personal. I just didn't want to get carried away.

"But then I got sick. And then I died. I mean, I died dead.

"Nothing left. Stone-cold. No life. No breath. Nothing. I died to everything. I saw life from the tomb. And then Jesus called me from the grave. When he spoke, my heart beat and my soul stirred, and I was alive again. And I want you to know he can do the same for you."

God gave Martha a bass drum of service. God gave Mary a flute for praise. And God gave Lazarus a trumpet. And he stood on center stage and played it.

God still gives trumpets. God still calls people from the pits. God still gives pinch-me-I'm-dreaming, too-good-to-be-true testimonies. But not everyone has a dramatic testimony. Who wants a band full of trumpets?

Some convert the lost. Some encourage the saved. And some keep the movement in step. All are needed.

If God has called you to be a Martha, then serve! Remind the rest of us that there is evangelism in feeding the poor and there is worship in nursing the sick.

If God has called you to be a Mary, then worship! Remind the rest of us that we don't have to be busy to be holy. Urge us with your example to put down our clipboards and megaphones and be quiet in worship.

If God has called you to be a Lazarus, then testify. Remind the rest of us that we, too, have a story to tell. We, too, have neighbors who are lost. We, too, have died and been resurrected.

Each of us has our place at the table.

Except one. There was one at Martha's house who didn't find his place. Though he had been near Jesus longer than any of the others, he was furthest in his faith. His name was Judas. He was a thief. When Mary poured the perfume he feigned spirituality. "The perfume could have been sold and given to the poor," he said. But Jesus knew Judas's heart, and Jesus defended Mary's worship. Years later, John, too, knew Judas's heart, and John explained that Judas was a thief (John 12:6). And all these years he had been dipping his hand in the treasury. The reason he wanted the perfume to be sold and the money put in the treasury was so that he could get his hands on it.

What a sad ending to a beautiful story. But what an appropriate ending. For in every church there are those like Martha who take time to serve. There are those like Mary who take time to worship. There are those like Lazarus who take time to testify.

And there are those like Judas who take, take, take, and never give in return. Are you a Judas? I ask the question carefully, yet honestly. Are you near Christ but far from his heart? Are you at the dinner with a sour soul? Are you always criticizing the gifts of others yet seldom, if ever, giving your own? Are you benefiting from the church while never giving to it? Do others give sacrificially while you give miserly? Are you a Judas?

Do you take, take, take, and never give? If so, you are the Judas in this story.

If you are a Martha, be strengthened. God sees your service.

If you are a Mary, be encouraged. God receives your worship.

If you are a Lazarus, be strong. God honors your conviction.

But if you are a Judas, be warned. God sees your selfishness.

The work God wants you to do is this: Believe in the One he sent.

John 6:29

Extravagant Love

Earn It or Receive It?

DISBELIEF HAS PECULIAR children:

There was the woman who was afraid to fly. After her flight she was asked if she had been nervous. "No," she responded. "I never sat down on the seat."

* * *

There was a king who left his servant in charge of the castle while he went on a journey. The king had a falcon. The servant had never seen a falcon and so when he saw the king's falcon, he thought it was a deformed pigeon. Out of compassion for the bird, he clipped its claws and filed its beak so it would look more like a pigeon.

* * *

There was a handsome prince who fell in love with a simple maiden. She wasn't attractive. She didn't trust his love. "How could you love me?" She would ask. "I'm not beautiful. I'm not rich. I'm not royalty."

"I just love you," he would answer.

He asked her to marry him. She still didn't trust his love, but she agreed. "I will marry you. I will clean your house and prepare your meals and bear your children."

"But I don't want to marry you for what you will do for me. I want to marry you because I love you."

And so they married. And so she cleaned his house and fixed his meals and bore his children. And he loved her. But she left him. She told a friend she didn't think he loved her anymore.

* * *

And so we have three people. Three people who couldn't believe. A woman who never enjoyed the flight because she couldn't trust the plane. A man who maimed a falcon because he'd never seen one. And a woman who lost the love of her life because she tried to earn what he wanted to give.

Disbelief has peculiar children. Children who are miserable on the journey, blind to the beauty, and oblivious to once-in-a-lifetime romance with God. Children who never fully relax in the palm of his grace. Children who forever trim and file at the splendor of his love. And children who hear his proposal but are always looking for the fine print and the hidden agenda.

The feelings of these children are captured in John 6:27–29. Jesus begins by saying: "Don't work for the food that spoils. Work for the food that stays good always and gives eternal life. The Son of Man will give you this food, because on him God the Father has put his power."

Jesus reduces the number of life's struggles to two. We either strive for food that rots or food that lasts. Food that rots is anything that is temporal: achievements, awards, applause . . . Any object that stays in the grave is a food that spoils.

Food that lasts, on the other hand, is anything that is eternal. And how do we get this food? Underline the promise, "The Son of Man will give you this food." You don't buy it, barter for it, or earn it. It is a gift. Just board the plane and sit down. Just unleash the falcon and watch it fly. Just accept his love and enjoy it . . .

Just believe.

But his listeners didn't get it. Look at their question: "What are the things God wants us to do?" (John 6:28). That, my friends, is the question of disbelief. "I know he said he would give it, but honestly now, how do we pay for this bread? How do we earn this meal? How long do we have to stand in the cafeteria line to get the eternal food?"

They missed the point. Didn't Jesus say, "The Son of Man will give you this food"?

Suppose I missed the point with you. Suppose you gave me a gift. Let's say you presented me with a new tie. I take it out of the box and examine it. I say thank you and then reach for my wallet. "Now how much do I owe you?" I ask.

You think I am kidding. "It's a gift," you say. "You don't need to pay me."

"Oh, I understand," I respond, but then show I don't by asking, "Could I write you a check?"

You're stunned. "I don't want you to pay me. I want you to accept the gift."

"Oh, I see," I respond. "Perhaps I could do some work around your house in exchange for the tie?"

"You just don't get it, do you?" you state firmly. "I want to give this to you. It is a present. You can't buy a present."

"Oh, forgive me," I hasten. "Perhaps if I promised to purchase you a tie in return."

By this time you're insulted. In trying to buy your gift I have degraded your grace. I have robbed you of the joy of giving.

How often we rob God.

Have you ever considered what an insult it is to God when we try to pay him for his goodness? God loves a cheerful giver because he is a cheerful giver. If we, who are evil, enjoy giving gifts, how much more does he? If we, who are human, are offended when people want to turn our gift into a bribe, how much more is God?

Spend some moments slowly reading the response of Jesus to their question, "What are the things God wants us to do?" (John 6:28).

Jesus replied: "The work God wants you to do is this . . ."

Can't you see the people lean closer, their minds racing? "What is the work he wants us to do? Pray more? Give more? Study? Travel? Memorize the Torah? What is the work he wants?" Sly is this scheme of Satan. Rather than lead us away from grace, he causes us to question grace or to earn it . . . and in the end we never even know it.

What is it, then, that God wants us to do? What is the work he seeks? Just believe. Believe the One he sent. "The work God wants you to do is this: Believe the One he sent."

Someone is reading this and shaking his or her head and asking, "Are you saying it is possible to go to heaven with no good works?" The answer is no. Good works are a requirement. Someone else is reading and asking, "Are you saying it is possible to go to heaven without good character?" My answer again is no. Good character is also required. In order to enter heaven one must have good works and good character.

But, alas, there is the problem. You have neither.

Oh, you've done some nice things in your life. But you do not have enough good works to go to heaven regardless of your sacrifice. No matter how noble your gifts, they are not enough to get you into heaven.

Nor do you have enough character to go to heaven. Please don't be offended. (Then, again, be offended, if necessary.) You're probably a very decent person. But decency isn't enough. Those who see God are not the decent; they are the holy. "Anyone whose life is not holy will never see the Lord" (Heb. 12:14).

You may be decent. You may pay taxes and kiss your kids and sleep with a clean conscience. But apart from Christ you aren't holy. So how can you go to heaven?

Only believe.

Accept the work already done, the work of Jesus on the cross.

Only believe.

Accept the goodness of Jesus Christ. Abandon your own works and accept his. Abandon your own decency and accept his. Stand before God in his name, not yours. "Anyone who believes and is baptized will be saved, but anyone who does not believe will be punished" (Mark 16:16).

It's that simple? It's that simple. It's that easy? There was nothing easy at all about it. The cross was heavy, the blood was real, and the price was extravagant. It would have bankrupted you or me, so he paid it for us. Call it simple. Call it a gift. But don't call it easy.

Call it what it is. Call it grace.

I have other sheep which are not of this flock and I must bring them also. They will listen to my voice, and there will be one flock and one shepherd.

John 10:16

Father, I pray that they can be one. . . . Then the world will know that you sent me and that you loved them as much as you loved me.

John 17:21, 23

God's Fondest Dream

Division or Unity

SOME TIME AGO I came upon a fellow on a trip who was carrying a Bible.

"Are you a believer?" I asked him.

"Yes," he said excitedly.

I've learned you can't be too careful.

"Virgin birth?" I asked.

"I accept it."

"Deity of Jesus?"

"No doubt."

"Death of Christ on the cross?"

"He died for all people."

Could it be that I was face to face with a Christian? Perhaps. Nonetheless, I continued my checklist.

"Status of man."

"Sinner in need of grace."

"Definition of grace."

"God doing for man what man can't do."

"Return of Christ?"

"Imminent."

"Bible?"

"Inspired."

"The church?"

"The body of Christ."

I started getting excited. "Conservative or liberal?"

He was getting interested too. "Conservative."

My heart began to beat faster.

"Heritage?"

"Southern Congregationalist Holy Son of God Dispensationalist Triune Convention."

That was mine!

"Branch?"

"Pre-millennial, post-trib, noncharismatic, King James, one-cup communion."

My eyes misted. I had only one other question.

"Is your pulpit wooden or fiberglass?"

"Fiberglass," he responded.

I withdrew my hand and stiffened my neck. "Heretic!" I said and walked away.

* * *

Far-fetched? If so, only a little. Suspicion and distrust often lurk at God's table. The Baptists distrust the Methodists. The Church of Christ avoids the Presbyterians. The Calvinists scoff at the Armenians. Charismatics. Immersionists. Patternists. Around the table the siblings squabble, and the Father sighs.

The Father sighs because he has a dream. "I have other sheep that are not in this flock, and I must bring them also. They will listen to my voice, and there will be one flock and one shepherd" (John 10:16).

God has only one flock. Somehow we missed that. Religious division is not his idea. Franchises and sectarianism are not in God's plan. God has one flock. The flock has one shepherd. And though we may think there are many, we are wrong. There is only one.

Never in the Bible are we told to create unity. We are simply told to maintain the unity that exists. Paul exhorts us to preserve "the unity which the Spirit gives" (Eph. 4:3, NEB). Our task is not to invent unity, but to acknowledge it.

I have two sisters and a brother. We are siblings because we came from the same family. We have the same father and mother. I'm sure there have been times when they didn't want to call me their brother, but they don't have that choice.

Nor do we. When I see someone calling God Father and Jesus Savior, I meet a brother or a sister—regardless of the name of their church or denomination.

By the way, the church names we banter about? They do not exist in heaven. The Book of Life does not list your denomination next to your name. Why? Because it is not the denomination that saves you. And I wonder, if there are no denominations in heaven, why do we have denominations on earth?

What would happen (I know this is a crazy thought), but what would happen if all the churches agreed, on a given day, to change their names to simply "church"? What if any reference to any denomination were removed and we were all just Christians? And then when people chose which church to attend, they wouldn't do so by the sign outside . . . they'd do so by the hearts of the people inside. And then when people were asked what church they attended, their answer wouldn't be a label but just a location.

And then we Christians wouldn't be known for what divides us; instead we'd be known for what unites us—our common Father.

Crazy idea? Perhaps.

But I think God would like it. It was his to begin with.

I am the true vine; my Father is the gardener. He cuts off every branch of mine that does not produce fruit. And he trims and cleans every branch that produces fruit so that it will produce even more fruit.

John 15:1–3

God's Been Known to Niggle

Do You Trust Him or Cuss Him?

EVERYONE LOVES WHAT Deborah Ricketts does. But nobody loves it while she's doing it. Everyone loves the product, but no one enjoys the process.

She is an independent researcher for the film industry. Do you want your movie to be accurate? Want your facts to be reliable? Send a script and a check to this former librarian and watch the facts begin to fly.

A film set in the thirties needs everything to look like the thirties. You can't have a person reading from a newspaper that didn't exist back then or a band playing a song that wasn't yet written. Such mistakes occur.

In *Raiders of the Lost Ark* the map that charted Indiana Jones's flight routed him over Thailand. Problem: The movie was set in 1936. Thailand was called Siam until 1939.

In *Die Hard II* Bruce Willis makes a phone call from what is supposed to be a Dulles Airport pay phone in Washington, D.C. No one noticed that the phone booth read Pacific Bell.

Deborah Ricketts lives to find these errors. She is on a scavenger hunt for flubs. She winds her way into props and sets and examines everything. Other people's oversights are her undertakings.[1]

She niggles for the scriptwriter's own good. The process is not pleasant, but the result is rewarding.

God has been known to niggle a few times, too. It's not that God loves to find fault. It's just that God loves to find anything that impedes our growth. Jesus portrays him as the Good Gardener who cuts and trims the vine. "I am the true vine; my Father is the gardener. He cuts off every branch of mine that does not produce fruit. And he trims and cleans every branch that produces fruit so that it will produce even more fruit" (John 15:1–3).

Jesus likely spoke these words while walking from the upper room to the Garden of Gethsemane. Perhaps he saw a vine hanging over a fence or draped along the wall. He lifted up a section of the plant and explained the chain of command in the universe. God is the Gardener. Jesus is the vine. We are the grapes.

Vines grew abundantly in Palestine. Carefully pruned, they produced sweet grapes. But left unkept, they crept everywhere and into everything. The gardener trimmed the vines. Why? So they could bear more fruit. God trims us. Why? For the same reason.

"I gave you this work," he explained, "to go and produce fruit, fruit that will last" (John 15:16).

A good gardener will do what it takes to help a vine bear fruit. What fruit does God want? Love, joy, peace, patience, kindness, goodness, faithfulness, gentleness, and self-control (see Gal. 5:22–23). These are the fruits of the Spirit. And this is what God longs to see in us. And like a careful gardener, he will clip and cut away anything that interferes.

A good track coach looks into the face of the runner and says, "We can break the record, but this is what it will take." And then the coach lists a regimen of practice and discipline.

A good editor reads the manuscript and says, "This work has potential, but here is what we need to cut." And the writer groans as the red ink flows.

A good piano instructor says, "I think you can master this piece for the competition, but to do so here is our rehearsal schedule." And the pianist sighs as she sees the hours required.

Deborah Rickets studies a script and offers: "It's good, but here are some ways to make it better."

God lifts up a branch of his vine and says, "You can be fruitful, but I'm going to have to clip some diseased leaves." And though the process is painful, we can see on the soil below us the spotted greenery he has clipped. Arrogance. Vain ambitions. Bad relationships. Dangerous opportunities. Revenge.

Does God take this process lightly? I don't think so. Listen to this serious statement. "He cuts off every branch of mine that does not produce fruit" (John 15:2). The verb "to cut off" is from the Greek word *airo*. It has at least two meanings; one is to "cut off," and the other is to "pick up" or "lift up." I believe both are implied.

Before God cuts a fruitless branch, he lifts it up. A gardener does this. He repositions the fruitless branch so it can get more sun or more space. Grapes are not like squash or pumpkins. They don't develop while lying on the ground. They grow better hanging free. A good vine dresser will stretch the vine on the arbor to afford it more air and sun.

You've seen gardeners realign a plant, and you've probably seen God realign a life. The family uprooted and transferred to another city—was it so they could learn to trust God? The person so healthy, suddenly sick—was it to remind him to rely on the Gardener? The income stream dried up—was it God's way of lifting you out of the soil of self and drawing you closer to himself? Leaders with questionable motives and morals are elected. Is it God's way of stirring people to revival?

God "does everything just right and on time, but people can never completely understand what he is doing" (Eccles. 3:11). (Did I just hear someone say "Amen"?) God is up to something. He is the busy, active Gardener who clears the field and removes the stones. He constructs the trellises and plants the seeds. He inspects the plants and pulls the weeds. And, most of all, he is good. He is the Good Gardener who cares for his vine.

So what are we to do? We branches on the vine, what is our response? How do we react? An answer commonly given at this point is the imperative, "Bear fruit!"

But is that the right response? Answer the question in a garden. If a branch is fruitless does it help if the gardener demands fruit? Or, if you are a branch, will you bear fruit by resolving to do so? You close your knobby eyes and grit your wooden teeth and strain until your bark turns red. Can you will a grape into existence? No. Please note, the branch cannot make fruit.

You cannot either. You've tried. With resolve in your eyes and grit in your jaw, you've tried. "Today I will be happy," you growl between clinched teeth.

Or, "I'm going to be patient, and I am going to be patient right now."

Or, "Okay, I'll be a cheerful giver. Give me that stupid collection plate."

Or, "I'm going to forgive that jerk if it kills me."

See what I mean? You can't force fruit. That's why nowhere in this text does Jesus tell you to go out and bear fruit.

What?

That's right. Nowhere does he command you to bear fruit. Go ahead, look. I did. It ain't there. Then what does he command us to do? Read John 15 for yourself:

"Remain in me . . ." (v. 4).

"Remain in the vine . . ." (v. 4).

"If any remain in me and I remain in them, they produce much fruit" (v. 5).

"Remain in me . . ." (v. 6).

"Remain in me . . ." (v. 7).

"Remain in my love . . ." (v. 9).

"Remain in my love . . ." (v. 10).

Our task? It's clear. Stay close to the vine. As long as we do, we'll be fruitful. Life comes through the vine. Apart from the vine, the branch does nothing. Jesus said it: "Apart from me you can do nothing" (John 15:5 NIV).

I doubt if it's easy for a scriptwriter to turn his manuscript over to someone like Deborah Rickets. He knows she's on the hunt for errors. But he also knows the end result will be a better story.

It's certainly not easy for us to turn our lives over to the gardener. Even now, some of you are hearing the snip-snip-snip of his shears. It hurts. But take heart. You'll be better as a result.

Besides, aren't you glad he thinks you are worth the effort?

I am the voice of the one calling out in the desert:
"Make the road straight for the Lord."

John 1:23

The Parable of the Sandwich Sign

Your Way or His?

THE FACES OF the three men were solemn as the mayor informed them of the catastrophe. "The rains have washed away the bridge. During the night many cars drove over the edge and into the river."

"What can we do?" asked one.

"You must stand on the side of the road and warn the drivers not to make the left turn. Tell them to take the one-lane road that follows the side of the river."

"But they drive so fast! How can we warn them?"

"By wearing these sandwich signs," the mayor explained, producing three wooden double-signs, hinged together to hang from one's shoulders. "Stand at the crossroads so drivers can see these signs until I can get someone out there to fix the bridge."

And so the men hurried out to the dangerous curve and put the signs over their shoulders.

"The drivers should see me first," spoke one. The others agreed. His sign warned, "Bridge Out!" He walked several hundred yards before the turn and took his post.

"Perhaps I should be second, so the drivers will slow down," spoke the one whose sign declared, "Reduce Speed."

"Good idea," agreed the third. "I'll stand here at the curve so people will get off the wide road and onto the narrow." His sign read simply "Take Right Road" and had a finger pointing toward the safe route.

And so the three men stood with their three signs ready to warn the travelers of the washed-out bridge. As the cars approached, the first man would stand up straight so the drivers could read, "Bridge Out."

Then the next would gesture to his sign, telling the cars to "Reduce Speed."

And as the motorists complied, they would then see the third sign, "Right Road Only." And though the road was narrow, the cars complied and were safe. Hundreds of lives were saved by the three sign holders. Because they did their job, many people were kept from peril.

But after a few hours they grew lax in their task.

The first man got sleepy. "I'll sit where people can read my sign as I sleep," he decided. So he took his sign off his shoulders and propped it up against a boulder. He leaned against it and fell asleep. As he slept his arm slid over the sign, blocking one of the two words. So rather than read "Bridge Out," his sign simply stated "Bridge."

The second didn't grow tired, but he did grow conceited. The longer he stood warning the people the more important he felt. A few even pulled off to the side of the road to thank him for the job well done.

"We might have died had you not told us to slow down," they applauded.

"You're so right," he thought to himself. "How many people would be lost were it not for me?"

Presently he came to think that he was just as important as his sign. So he took it off, set it up on the ground, and stood beside it. As he did, he was unaware that he, too, was blocking one word of his warning. He was standing in front of the word "Speed." All the drivers could read was the word "Reduce." Most thought he was advertising a diet plan.

The third man was not tired like the first, nor self-consumed like the second. But he was concerned about the message of his sign. "Right Road Only," it read.

It troubled him that his message was so narrow, so dogmatic. "People should be given a choice in the matter. Who am I to tell them which is the right road and which is the wrong road?"

So he decided to alter the wording of the sign. He marked out the word "Only" and changed it to "Preferred."

"Hmm," he thought, "that's still too strident. One is best not to moralize. So he marked out the word "Preferred" and wrote "Suggested."

That still didn't seem right, "Might offend people if they think I'm suggesting I know something they don't."

So he thought and thought and finally marked through the word "Suggested" and replaced it with a more neutral phrase.

"Ahh, just right," he said to himself as he backed off and read the words:

"Right Road—One of Two Equally Valid Alternatives."

And so as the first man slept and the second stood and the third altered the message, one car after another plunged into the river.

*He is the One who comes after me. I am not good
enough to tie the strings of his sandals.*

John 1:27

The Winsomeness of Holiness

Leading or Misleading?

JOHN THE BAPTIST would never get hired today. No church would touch him. He was a public relations disaster. He "wore clothes made from camel's hair, had a leather belt around his waist, and ate locusts and wild honey" (Mark 1:6). Who would want to look at a guy like that every Sunday?

His message was as rough as his dress: a no-nonsense, bare-fisted challenge to repent because God was on his way.

Didn't matter to John if you were a Jew, a priest, a Baptist, or all three. What mattered was that you get off your duff and get right with God because he's coming and he don't mean maybe.

No, John would never get hired today. His tactics lacked tact. His style wasn't smooth. He made few friends and lots of enemies, but what do you know? He made hundreds of converts. "All the people from Judea and Jerusalem were going out to him. They confessed their sins and were baptized by him in the Jordan River" (Mark 1:5).

Look at that. "All the people of Judea and Jerusalem. . . ." How do we explain such a response? It certainly wasn't his charisma or clothing. Nor was it his money or position, for he had neither. Then what did he have?

One word. *Holiness.*

John the Baptist set himself apart for one task, to be a voice of Christ. Everything about John centered on his purpose. His dress. His diet. His actions. His demands.

He reminded his hearers of Elijah. And he reminds us of this truth: "There is winsomeness in holiness." You don't have to be like the world to have an impact on the world. You don't have to be like the crowd to change the crowd. You don't have to lower yourself down to their level to lift them up to your level.

Nor do you have to be weird. You don't need to wear camel's-hair clothing or eat insects. Holiness doesn't seek to be odd. Holiness seeks to be like God.

You want to make a difference in your world? Live a holy life:

Be faithful to your spouse.

Be the one at the office who refuses to cheat.

Be the neighbor who acts neighborly.

Be the employee who does the work and doesn't complain.

Pay your bills.

Do your part and enjoy life.

Don't speak one message and live another.

Note the last line of Paul's words in 1 Thessalonians 4:11–12.

> Do all you can to lead a peaceful life. Take care of your own business, and do your own work as we have already told you. If you do, then people who are not believers will respect you.

A peaceful life leads nonbelievers to respect believers. What if John's life had not matched his words? What if he'd preached repentance and lived in immorality? What if he'd called for holiness and yet had a reputation for dishonesty? If John's life had not matched his words, his message would have fallen on deaf ears.

So will ours.

People are watching the way we act more than they are listening to what we say.

Saint Francis of Assisi once invited a young monk to accompany him to town to preach. The novice was honored at the opportunity.

The two set out for the city, then walked up and down the main street, then several side streets. They chatted with peddlers and greeted the citizens. After some time they returned by another route to the abbey.

The younger man reminded Francis of his original intent. "You have forgotten, Father, that we went to town to preach."

"My son," he replied, "we have preached. We have been seen by many. Our behavior was closely watched. Our attitudes were closely measured. Our words have been overheard. It was by thus that we preached our morning sermon."[1]

John was a voice for Christ with more than his voice. His life matched his words. When a person's ways and words are the same, the fusion is explosive. But when a person says one thing and lives another, the result is destructive. People will know we are Christians, not because we bear the name, but because we live the life.

It's the life that earns the name, not the name that creates the life. Here's a story that illustrates this point.

A Jewish couple were arguing over the name to give their firstborn. They finally asked the rabbi to come and intercede.

"What is the problem?" the rabbi asked.

The wife spoke first. "He wants to name the boy after his father, and I want to name the boy after my father."

"What is your father's name?" he asked the man.

"Joseph."

"And what is your father's name?" he asked the woman.

"Joseph."

The rabbi was stunned. "So, what is the problem?"

It was the wife who spoke again. "His father was a horse thief, and mine was a righteous man. How can I know my son is named after my father and not his?"

The rabbi thought and then replied, "Call the boy Joseph. Then see if he is a horse thief or a righteous man. You will know which father's name he wears."

To call yourself a child of God is one thing. To be called a child of God by those who watch your life is another thing altogether.

As Jesus was walking along, he saw a man who had been born blind. His followers asked him, "Teacher, whose sin caused this man to be born blind— his own sin or his parents' sin?"

John 9:1–2

Look Before You Label
Caring or Condemning?

RECENTLY WE TOOK our kids on a vacation to a historical city. While going on a tour through an old house, we followed a family from New York City. They didn't tell me they were from New York. They didn't have to. I could tell. They wore New York City clothes. Their teenager had one half of his head shaved and on the other half of his head, his hair hung past his shoulders. The daughter wore layered clothes and long beads. The mother looked like she'd raided her daughter's closet, and the dad's hair was down the back of his neck.

I had them all figured out. The kid was probably on drugs. The parents were going through a midlife crisis. They were rich and miserable and in need of counseling. Good thing I was nearby in case they wanted spiritual counsel.

After a few moments they introduced themselves. I was right; they were from New York City. But that is all I got right. When I told them my name, they were flabbergasted. "We can't believe it!" they said. "We've read your books. We use them in our Sunday school class in church. I tried to get over to hear you when you spoke in our area, but that was our family night and . . ."

Sunday school? Church? Family night? Oh, boy. I'd made a mistake. A big mistake. I'd applied the label before examining the contents.

We've all used labels. We stick them on jars and manila folders so we'll know what's inside. We also stick them on people for the same reason.

John tells of a time the disciples applied a label. Jesus and his followers came upon a man who had been blind from birth. Here is the question the disciples asked Jesus: "Teacher, whose sin caused this man to be born blind—his own sin or his parents' sin?" (John 9:2).

Never mind that the man is a beggar in need of help. Never mind that the man has spent his life in a dark cave. Never mind that the man seated in front of them is in earshot of their voices. Let's talk about his sin.

How could they be so harsh? So insensitive? So . . . blind.

The answer? (You may not like it.) It's easier to talk about a person than to help a person. It's easier to debate homosexuality than to be a friend to a gay person. It's easier to discuss divorce than to help the divorced. It's easier to argue abortion than to support an orphanage. It's easier to complain about the welfare system than to help the poor.

It's easier to label than to love.

It's especially easy to talk theology. Such discussions make us feel righteous. Self-righteous.

As long as I'm confessing sins, I might as well confess another. We had such a theological discussion in Brazil. We missionaries debated whether we should offer Communion to people who are not members of our church. Our reasoning? What if they aren't faithful? What if they aren't truly converted? What if their hearts aren't right? If we offer them Communion, we could be leading them to eat the bread or drink of the cup in an unworthy manner, thereby leading them to sin (see 1 Cor. 11:27). So we decided that first-time visitors could not partake.

We meant well. It sounded right. But I learned a lesson.

Guess what happened. That very week a friend told me he would like to visit the church. The same friend we had been inviting for weeks. The same friend who had shown no interest was suddenly interested. At first I was elated; then my heart sank. I told him he could come, but he couldn't partake of Communion.

As long as I live, I'll never forget the look on his face as he passed the Communion plate to the person next to him. He never returned. Who could blame him? We'd applied the label before we looked inside.

Is that to say religious discussion is wrong? Of course not. Is that to say we should be unconcerned for doctrine or lax in a desire for holiness? Absolutely not. That is to say there is something wrong with applying the label before examining the contents. Do you like it when people label you before they know you?

"So, you're unemployed?" (Translation: *Must be a bum.*)

"Hmm, you're an accountant?" (Translation: *Must be dull.*)

"She's an Episcopalian." (Translation: *Must be liberal.*)

"She's an Episcopalian who voted for the democrats." (Translation: *Must be liberal beyond help.*)

"Oh, I'm sorry; I didn't know you were a divorcee." (Translation: *Must be immoral.*)

"He's a fundamentalist." (Translation: *Narrow-minded half-wit.*)

Labels. A fellow gave me one the other day. We got into a lively discussion about some ethical issues. Somewhere in our conversation he asked me what kind of work I was in. I told him I was minister, and he said, "Oh, I see," and grew silent.

I wanted to say, "No, you don't. Don't you put me in that box. I'm not a minister. I am Max-who-ministers. Don't you put me in that box with all those hucksters and hypocrites you may know. That's not fair."

Labels. So convenient. Stick them on a person, and you know what pantry to use.

What if God did that with us? What if God judged us by our outward appearance? What if he judged us based on where we grew up? Or what we do for a living? Or the mistakes we made when we were young? He wouldn't do that, would he?

"Don't judge other people, or you will be judged. You will be judged in the same way you judge others, and the amount you give to others will be given to you" (Matt. 7:1–2).

Be careful when you judge. That doesn't mean we shouldn't discern. That does mean we shouldn't pass the verdict. The amount of grace you give is the amount you get.

Jesus had another view of the man born blind. Rather than see him as an opportunity for discussion, he saw him as an opportunity for God. Why was he blind? "So God's power could be shown in him" (John 9:3).

What a perspective! The man wasn't a victim of fate; he was a miracle waiting to happen. Jesus didn't label him. He helped him. Jesus was more concerned about the future than the past.

Who do you best relate to in this story? Some of you relate to the man born blind. You have been the topic of conversation. You have been left on the outside looking in. You've been labeled.

If so, learn what this man learned: When everyone else rejects you, Christ accepts you. When everyone else leaves you, Christ finds you. When no one else wants you, Christ claims you. When no one else will give you the time of day, Jesus will give you the words of eternity.

Others of you will relate to the observers. You've judged. You've labeled. You've slammed the gavel and proclaimed the guilt before knowing the facts. If that is you, go back to John 9:4 and understand what the work of God is: "While it is daytime we must continue doing the work of the One who sent me."

What is the work of God? Accepting people. Loving before judging. Caring before condemning.

Look before you label.

Then some of the people who lived in Jerusalem said, . . . "We know where this man is from. And when the real Christ comes, no one will know where he comes from."

John 7:25–27

26

Looking for the Messiah

How Do You See Him?

SUPPOSE JESUS CAME to your church. I don't mean symbolically. I mean visibly. Physically. Actually. Suppose he came to your
church.

Would you recognize him? It might be difficult. Jesus didn't wear
religious clothes in his day. Doubtful that he would wear them in ours.
If he came today to your church, he'd wear regular clothes. Nothing
fancy, just a jacket and shoes and a tie. Maybe a tie . . . maybe not.

He would have a common name. "Jesus" was common. I suppose he might go by Joe or Bob or Terry or Elliot.

Elliot . . . I like that. Suppose Elliot, the Son of God, came to
your church.

Of course, he wouldn't be from Nazareth or Israel. He'd hail
from some small spot down the road like Hollow Point or Chester
City or Mt. Pleasant.

And he'd be a laborer. He was a carpenter in his day. No reason
to think he'd change, but let's say he did. Let's say that this time
around he was a plumber. Elliot, the plumber from Mt. Pleasant.

God, a plumber?

Rumor has it that he fed a football field full of people near the
lake. Others say he healed a senator's son from Biloxi. Some say

he's the Son of God. Others say he's the joke of the year. You don't know what to think.

And then, one Sunday, he shows up.

About midway through the service he appears in the back of the auditorium and takes a seat. After a few songs he moves closer to the front. After yet another song he steps up on the platform and announces, "You are singing about me. I am the Son of God." He holds a Communion tray. "This bread is my body. This wine is my blood. When you celebrate this, you celebrate me!"

What would you think?

Would you be offended? *The audacity of it all. How irreverent, a guy named Elliot as the Son of God!*

Would you be interested? *Wait a minute, how could he be the Son of God? He never went to seminary, never studied at a college. But there is something about him . . .*

Would you believe? *I can't deny it's crazy. But I can't deny what he has done.*

It's easy to criticize contemporaries of Jesus for not believing in him. But when you realize how he came, you can understand their skepticism.

Jesus didn't fit their concept of a Messiah. Wrong background. Wrong pedigree. Wrong hometown. No Messiah would come from Nazareth. Small, hick, one-stoplight town. He didn't fit the Jews' notion of a Messiah, and so, rather than change their notion, they dismissed him.

He came as one of them. He was Jesus from Nazareth. Elliot from Mt. Pleasant. He fed the masses with calloused hands. He raised the dead wearing bib overalls and a John Deere Tractor cap.

They expected lights and kings and chariots from heaven. What they got was sandals and sermons and a Galilean accent.

And so, some missed him.

And so, some miss him still.

We have our own preconceptions, don't we? We still think we know which phone God uses and which car he drives. We still think we know what he looks like. But he's been known to surprise us.

We expect God to speak through peace, but sometimes he speaks through pain.

We think God talks through the church, but he also talks through the lost.

We look for the answer among the Protestants, but he's been known to speak through the Catholics.

We listen for him among the Catholics but find him among the Quakers.

We think we hear him in the sunrise, but he is also heard in the darkness.

We listen for him in triumph, but he speaks even more distinctly through tragedy.

We must let God define himself.

We must put away our preconceptions; otherwise we'll make the same mistake a lady in Baltimore made recently. Our radio ministry was hosting a radio rally. After my talk, I stayed around to meet the folks who listen to my program. These people had never seen me, but they had heard my voice. Presently a small, elderly woman stepped up.

"You don't look like you," was her first statement.

"Excuse me?"

"You don't look like you. Max Lucado is older, and his hair is grayer."

I hated to disappoint the lady, but she was wrong. I looked just like me. My face would match the picture on my driver's license, but that didn't matter to her. She wanted a face to match her preconception.

She had an image in her mind that didn't match the image she saw. She had to make a choice. She had to accept the true me or live with the wrong impression. We must do the same with God.

When we do, when we let God define himself, a whole new world opens before us. How, you ask? Let me explain with a story.

Once there was a man whose life was one of misery. The days were cloudy, and the nights were long. Henry didn't want to be unhappy, but he was. With the passing of the years, his life had changed. His children were grown. The neighborhood was different. The city seemed harsher.

He was unhappy. He decided to ask his minister what was wrong.

"Am I unhappy for some sin I have committed?"

"Yes," the wise pastor replied. "You have sinned."

"And what might that sin be?"

"Ignorance," came the reply. "The sin of ignorance. One of your neighbors is the Messiah in disguise, and you have not seen him."

The old man left the office stunned. "The Messiah is one of my neighbors?" He began to think who it might be.

Tom the butcher? No, he's too lazy. Mary, my cousin down the street? No, too much pride. Aaron the paperboy? No, too indulgent. The man was confounded. Every person he knew had defects. But one was the Messiah. He began to look for Him.

He began to notice things he hadn't seen. The grocer often carried sacks to the cars of older ladies. *Maybe he is the Messiah.* The officer at the corner always had a smile for the kids. *Could it be?* And the young couple who'd moved next door. *How kind they are to their cat. Maybe one of them . . .*

With time he saw things in people he'd never seen. And with time his outlook began to change. The bounce returned to his step. His eyes took on a friendly sparkle. When others spoke he listened. After all, he might be listening to the Messiah. When anyone asked for help, he responded; after all this might be the Messiah needing assistance.

The change of attitude was so significant that someone asked him why he was so happy. "I don't know," he answered. "All I know is that things changed when I started looking for God."

Now, that's curious. The old man saw Jesus because he didn't know what he looked like. The people in Jesus' day missed him because they thought they did.

How are things looking in your neighborhood?

As Simon Peter was standing and warming him-
self, they said to him, "Aren't you one of that man's
followers?" Peter said it was not true; he said, "No, I
am not."

One of the servants of the high priest was there.
This servant was a relative of the man whose ear
Peter had cut off. The servant said, "Didn't I see you
with him in the garden?"

Again Peter said it wasn't true. At once the rooster
crowed.

John 18:25–27

Peter, Me, and Wile E. Coyote

Guilt or Grace?

WILE E. COYOTE furiously chases Roadrunner. The bird suddenly stops. The coyote tries to but can't, and he skids past the roadrunner out to the edge of a cliff. The ground gives way and for just a moment we see his saucer eyes. Then down Wile E. plummets. *Poof!*

I love to watch old *Roadrunner* cartoons. Wile E. Coyote and I share a common plight. I, too, have ventured too close to the edge. I've found myself on shaky ground and taken a fall. I've stared that "oh-boy-this-is-gonna-hurt" stare. I've looked up from the bottom of the pit, dazed and stunned.

But Wile E. has something I don't. He's invincible. He never gets hurt. The falls don't faze him. In the next scene of the cartoon he's stacking Acme dynamite or painting a wall to make it appear like a tunnel. Within moments, he's out of the pit, back on the trail.

You and I don't recover so easily. Like Wile E., we fall. But unlike Wile E., we wander in the canyon for a while. Stunned, hurt . . . and wondering if this ravine has a way out.

Few of us have been in a pit deeper than Peter's. Which is ironic, for just an hour or two before, he was high on the pinnacle and far from the pit. "Simon Peter, who had a sword, pulled it out and struck the servant of the high priest, cutting off his right ear" (John 18:10).

Smugly, Peter stands next to Jesus, flashing his sword. "Step aside, Jesus, I'll take care of this one for you." My hunch is Peter expected a fight. My hunch is Peter was stunned when Jesus told him to put away his sword. Next thing Peter knows, the Savior and the soldiers are headed down the hill and Peter's alone with his decision. Does he stick close to Jesus or duck in the shadows? He opts to do neither.

Luke tells us that Peter followed Jesus and his captors from a distance (see Luke 22:54). Not too close, yet not too far. Near enough to see him, but not near enough to be seen with him. Love made Peter ashamed to run; fear made him ashamed to draw near. The disciples chose the left side of the road and ran. Jesus chose the right side of the road and obeyed. But Peter chose the yellow stripe down the middle. BIG mistake.

He would have been better off in the shadows with the disciples. He would have been better off in the courtyard with his master. But instead Peter is warming his hands on the devil's hearth. A young girl recognizes him and asks, "Aren't you one of that man's followers?"

"No, I am not!" he defies.

Moments later he is asked the question again: "Aren't you one of the man's followers?" And a second time he denies his Lord. The third question comes from a relative of Malchus: "Didn't I see you with him in the garden?" This time Peter curses the very thought of it (Matt. 26:74).

With each denial Peter inches closer to the edge of the canyon . . . until the ground gives way and he falls.

Have you been there? Have you felt the ground of conviction give way beneath your feet? The ledge crumbles, your eyes widen, and down you go. *Poof!*

Now what do you do? You could stay in the canyon. Many do. Many live their lives in the shadows. Many never return. Some dismiss their deeds. "Well, everybody has a little slip now and then."

Some deny their deeds. "Fall? Me? Are you kidding? These aren't bruises. These aren't cuts. I'm as healthy as I've ever been. Me and Jesus? We are tight." Some distort their deeds. "I'm not to blame. It's his fault. It's society's responsibility. If the people hadn't asked me, I wouldn't have answered. Don't point the finger at me."

When we fall, we can dismiss it. We can deny it. We can distort it. Or we can deal with it.

Luke adds a chilling phrase to his account of Peter's denial of Christ. When the cock crowed, "the Lord turned and looked straight at Peter" (Luke 22:61).

The rooster reminds Peter of Jesus' warning. Peter lifts his eyes and looks across the courtyard, only to find Jesus looking at him. Jesus is being assailed by accusations, but he doesn't hear them. He hears only the denial of his friend.

If Peter ever thought he could keep his fall a secret, he now knows he can't. "Nothing in all the world can be hidden from God. Everything is clear and lies open before him, and to him we must explain the way we have lived" (Heb. 4:13).

We keep no secrets from God. Confession is not telling God what we did. He already knows. Confession is simply agreeing with God that our acts were wrong. Did Peter do this? Again let Luke speak: "And Peter remembered what the Lord had said: 'Before the rooster crows this day you will say three times that you don't know me.' Then Peter went outside and cried painfully" (Luke 22:61–62).

Each tear a confession, each sob an admission, Peter remembers the words of Jesus and weeps.

There is an old story about the time Emperor Frederick the Great visited Potsdam Prison. He spoke with the prisoners, and each man claimed to be innocent, a victim of the system. One man, however, sat silently in the corner.

The ruler asked him, "And you, sir, who do you blame for your sentence?"

His response was, "Your majesty, I am guilty and richly deserve my punishment." Surprised, the emperor shouted for the prison warden: "Come and get this man out of here before he corrupts all these innocent people."[1]

The ruler can set us free once we admit we are wrong.

We do ourselves no favors in justifying our deeds or glossing over our sins. Some time ago my daughter Andrea got a splinter in her finger. I took her to the restroom and set out some tweezers, ointment, and a Band-Aid.

She didn't like what she saw. "I just want the Band-Aid, Daddy."

Sometimes we are just like Andrea. We come to Christ with our sin, but all we want is a covering. We want to skip the treatment. We want to hide our sin. And one wonders if God, even in his great mercy, will heal what we conceal. "If we say we have no sin, we are fooling ourselves, and the truth is not in us. But if we confess our sins, he will forgive our sins, because we can trust God to do what is right" (1 John 1:8–9).

Going to God is not going to Santa Claus. A child sits on the chubby lap of Ol' Saint Nick and Santa pinches the youngster's cheek and asks, "Have you been a good little girl?"

"Yes," she giggles. Then she tells him what she wants and down she bounds. It's a game. It's childish. No one takes Santa's question seriously. That may work in a department store, but it won't work with God.

How can God heal what we deny? How can God touch what we cover up? How can we have communion while we keep secrets? How can God grant us pardon when we won't admit our guilt?

Ahh, there's that word: *guilt*. Isn't that what we avoid? Guilt. Isn't that what we detest? But is guilt so bad? What does guilt imply if not that we know right from wrong, that we aspire to be better than we are, that we know there is a high country and we are in the low country. That's what guilt is: a healthy regret for telling God one thing and doing another.

Guilt is the nerve-ending of the heart. It yanks us back when we are too near the fire. Godly sorrow "makes people change their hearts and lives. This leads to salvation, and you cannot be sorry for that" (2 Cor. 7:10).

To feel guilt is no tragedy; to feel no guilt is.

When Peter saw Jesus looking at him from across the courtyard, he was flooded with guilt.

What if Peter hadn't dealt with his feelings of guilt? What if Peter had dismissed, denied, or distorted his sin? What if he had never exited the canyon? How many sermons would have gone unpreached? How many lives would have gone untouched or epistles gone unwritten?

Had Peter not felt the guilt in the courtyard, he never would have proclaimed the grace on Pentecost. Had Peter not left the canyon, he never would have shared the Christ.

Which leads us to wonder how many untold stories walk the canyon floor today . . . How many lives have been neutralized by guilt? How many Peters are in the shadows, wanting to come out, if only they knew the way.

Peter shows the way.

Please note, there are two fires in Peter's story. The first is the fire of denial, but the second is the fire of discovery. The first fire was built by men; the second was built by Christ. At the first fire, Peter denied Jesus. At the second, Peter confessed him.

What took Peter from one fire to the next? How did he journey from the fire of denial to the fire of discovery? In between the fires are two events: the tears of Peter and the cross of Jesus. Both are essential. If Peter had shed tears but not seen the cross, he would have known only despair. Had he seen the cross but shed no tears, he would have known only arrogance. But since he saw both, he knew redemption.

Mingle the tears of the sinner with the cross of the Savior and the result is a joyful escort out of the canyon of guilt.

There are many rooms in my Father's house; I would not tell you this if it were not true. I am going there to prepare a place for you.

John 14:2

Ready for Home
Ready or Not

HAD YOU BEEN on the British Coast in 1845 you might have seen two ships boarded by 138 of England's finest sailors setting sail for the Arctic. Their task? To chart the Northwest Passage around the Canadian Arctic to the Pacific Ocean.

The captain, Sir John Franklin, hoped this effort would be the turning point in Arctic exploration. History shows that it was. Not because of its success, but because of its failure. The ships never returned. Every crew member perished. And those who followed in the expedition's path to the pole learned this lesson: Prepare for the journey.

Apparently Franklin didn't. Though the voyage was projected to last two or three years, he only carried a twelve-day supply of coal for the auxiliary steam engines. But what he lacked in fuel, he made up for in entertainment. Each ship carried a "1,200 volume library, a hand-organ, china place settings for officers and men, cut-glass wine goblets and sterling silver flatware."[1]

Was the crew planning for an Arctic expedition or a Caribbean cruise? Judging from the supplies, one would have thought the latter. The sailors carried no special clothing to protect them against the cold. Only the uniforms of Her Majesty's fleet. Noble and respectful, but thin and inadequate.

The silver knives, forks, and spoons were as ornate as those found in the dining rooms of the Royal Navy officers clubs: heavy at the handles, intricately designed. Years later, some of these place settings would be found near a clump of frozen, cannibalized bodies.

The inevitable had occurred. The two ships had sailed ill-prepared into the frigid waters. Ice coated the deck, the spars, and the rigging. The sea froze around the rudder and trapped the ship.

The sailors set out to search for help, wearing their uniforms and carrying their belongings. Inuit Indians reported seeing a group dragging a wooden boat across the ice. For the next twenty years, remains of the expedition were found all over the frozen sea. The boat, or a similar one, was later discovered containing the bodies of thirty-five men. Other Indians discovered a tent on the ice and in it, thirty bodies.

Franklin died on the boat. Search parties would later find a piece of the backgammon board Lady Jane Franklin had given her husband as a farewell present.

Many miles from the vessel, the skeleton of a frozen officer was discovered, still wearing trousers and jacket of "fine blue cloth . . . edged with silk braid, with sleeves slashed and bearing five buttons each. Over his uniform the dead man had worn a blue greatcoat, with a black silk neckerchief."[2]

Strange how men could embark on such a journey ill-prepared, more equipped for afternoon tea than for the open sea.

Stranger still how we do the same. Don't Franklin's men remind you of us? We sometimes act as if the Christian life is a retirement cruise. We have little fuel but lots of entertainment. We are more concerned with looking snappy than with being prepared. We give more thought to table settings than to surviving the journey. We give little thought to the destination, but we make sure there's plenty of silver to go around.

And so when the freeze comes, we step out on the ice with forks, games, and skimpy clothing and pass our final days walking against the wind, often blaming God for getting us into this mess.

But God is not to blame. If we sail unprepared it's in spite of—not because of—God. He left detailed instructions about this voyage. His Word is our map; the Holy Spirit is our compass.

He outlined the route and described the landmarks we should seek.

He even told us what to pack for the trip: love, joy, peace, patience, kindness, goodness, faithfulness, gentleness, self-control (see Gal. 5:22–23).

And most remarkably, he's gone before us and goes with us. He's both a pioneer and a co-traveler! And when we grow weary, all we need to do is listen to his voice. He's got special promises to keep us on the journey.

Here is one of the best.

"There are many rooms in my father's house."

What a tender phrase. A house implies rest, safety, warmth, a table, a bed, a place to be at home. But this isn't just any house. It is our Father's house.

All of us know what it is like to be in a house that is not our own. Perhaps you've spent time in a dorm room or army barrack. Maybe you've slept in your share of hotels or bunked in a few hostels. They have beds. They have tables. They may have food and they may be warm, but they are a far cry from being "your father's house."

Your father's house is where your father is.

Perhaps you can remember the voice of your father? Coming home from work filling the hallways? Sounding through the rooms? Some of you can. And for many, the memory is fond.

Others of you don't have that memory, but you will. "If my father and mother leave me, the LORD will take me in" (Ps. 27:10).

Your Father is preparing a place for you. A place with *many* rooms. An ample place. A place with space for you. There is a special room for you. You will be welcome.

We don't always feel welcome here on earth. We wonder if there is a place here for us. People can make us feel unwanted. Tragedy leaves us feeling like intruders. Strangers. Interlopers in a land not ours. We don't always feel welcome here.

We shouldn't. This isn't our home. To feel unwelcome is no tragedy. Indeed it is healthy. We are not home here. This language we speak, it's not ours. This body we wear, it isn't us. And the world we live in, this isn't home.

Ours isn't finished yet.

But when it is, our brother will come and take us home. "I would not tell you this if it were not true. . . . I will come back," he said before he left, "and take you to be with me so that you may be where I am" (John 14:2–3).

That first sentence is a curious one. "*I would not tell you this if it were not true*." Why did he say that? Did he see doubt in the heart of the disciples? Did he read confusion on their faces? I don't know what he saw in their eyes. But I know what he sees in ours.

He sees what the airline attendant sees when she gives her preflight warnings.

He sees what physicians often see when they tell patients to stop smoking.

He sees what ministers see when they tell a Sunday morning audience that each one of them could die today.

"*Yeah, sure. But probably not.*"

We don't say the words. But we think them. Sure, this plane could crash, but then again it probably won't. *So rather than listen I'll read my magazine. Sure I could die of cancer, but then again, maybe I won't. So rather than stop smoking today I'll wait awhile. Sure I could die today, but then again . . .*

General William Nelson was a Union general in the Civil War. Though he faced death every day, he never prepared for his own. Who knows what he was thinking as he rode into battle after battle? Maybe he was too busy staying alive to prepare for death.

All that changed, however, one day as he was relaxing in a house with his men. A brawl broke out, and he was shot in the chest. Knowing he was dying, he had only one request: "Send for a clergyman."

What had happened? Why the urgency? Did the general suddenly learn something about God that he had never known? No.

But he did learn something about himself. He realized death was near. Suddenly only one thing mattered.[3]

Why hadn't it mattered before? Couldn't he have said yes to God the week before or that very morning? Absolutely. Why didn't he? Why was the salvation of his soul so urgent after the shot and so optional before it? Why had he postponed his decision to accept Christ until his deathbed?

Because he assumed he had time.

A dangerous assumption. "Teach us how short our lives really are," prayed Moses, "so that we may be wise" (Ps. 90:12).

What fear strikes a man when the end is near and he's not prepared.

What fear must have struck the crew of Sir John Franklin when they became stuck in the ice. What anxiety to search for food and find silver, to dig in the closets for coats and find uniforms, to explore the ship for picks and axes and find backgammon games and novels.

Don't you know they would have swapped it all in a heartbeat for what they needed to get home safely?

By the way, what supplies are you taking? Are you carrying your share of silver and games? Don't be fooled; they may matter here, but they matter not when you reach your Father's house. What matters is if you are known by the Father.

It's not what you have; it's who you know. Be prepared. You don't want to be left out in the cold.

He came to the world that was his own, but his own people did not accept him.

John 1:11

The Cave People
Will You Share the Light?

LONG AGO, OR maybe not so long ago, there was a tribe in a dark, cold cavern.

The cave dwellers would huddle together and cry against the chill. Loud and long they wailed. It was all they did. It was all they knew to do. The sounds in the cave were mournful, but the people didn't know it, for they had never known joy. The spirit in the cave was death, but the people didn't know it, for they had never known life.

But then, one day, they heard a different voice. "I have heard your cries," it announced. "I have felt your chill and seen your darkness. I have come to help."

The cave people grew quiet. They had never heard this voice. Hope sounded strange to their ears. "How can we know you have come to help?"

"Trust me," he answered. "I have what you need."

The cave people peered through the darkness at the figure of the stranger. He was stacking something, then stooping and stacking more.

"What are you doing?" one cried, nervous.

The stranger didn't answer.

"What are you making?" one shouted even louder.

Still no response.

"Tell us!" demanded a third.

The visitor stood and spoke in the direction of the voices. "I have what you need." With that he turned to the pile at his feet and lit it. Wood ignited, flames erupted, and light filled the cavern.

The cave people turned away in fear. "Put it out!" they cried. "It hurts to see it."

"Light always hurts before it helps," he answered. "Step closer. The pain will soon pass."

"Not I," declared a voice.

"Nor I," agreed a second.

"Only a fool would risk exposing his eyes to such light."

The stranger stood next to the fire. "Would you prefer the darkness? Would you prefer the cold? Don't consult your fears. Take a step of faith."

For a long time no one spoke. The people hovered in groups covering their eyes. The fire builder stood next to the fire. "It's warm here," he invited.

"He's right," one from behind him announced. "It's warmer." The stranger turned and saw a figure slowly stepping toward the fire. "I can open my eyes now," she proclaimed. "I can see."

"Come closer," invited the fire builder.

She did. She stepped into the ring of light. "It's so warm!" She extended her hands and sighed as her chill began to pass.

"Come, everyone! Feel the warmth," she invited.

"Silence, woman!" cried one of the cave dwellers. "Dare you lead us into your folly? Leave us. Leave us and take your light with you."

She turned to the stranger. "Why won't they come?"

"They choose the chill, for though it's cold, it's what they know. They'd rather be cold than change."

"And live in the dark?"

"And live in the dark."

The now-warm woman stood silent. Looking first at the dark, then at the man.

"Will you leave the fire?" he asked.

She paused, then answered, "I cannot. I cannot bear the cold." Then she spoke again. "But nor can I bear the thought of my people in darkness."

"You don't have to," he responded, reaching into the fire and removing a stick. "Carry this to your people. Tell them the light is here, and the light is warm. Tell them the light is for all who desire it."

And so she took the small flame and stepped into the shadows.

I have good plans for you, not plans to hurt you. I will give you hope and a good future.

Jeremiah 29:11

If Only You Knew

WHAT I INTENDED as good was interpreted as bad . . . by a hummingbird.

Dozens of the little fellows linger around our house. It's a cordial relationship. We provide the nectar, and they provide the amusement.

Yesterday one of them got into trouble. He flew into the garage and got lost. Though the door was open for him to exit, he didn't see it. He insisted, instead, on bashing his head against a closed window. He was determined to get out, but his determination would not break the glass.

Soon our whole family was in the garage, empathizing with his confusion. "Help him out, Daddy," came the chorus from my kids.

So I tried. I raised the window, hoping he'd fly out—he didn't. He rode the frame as it rose. I nudged him with a broom handle, hoping he'd fly though the open window below. He didn't. I bumped him harder. He wouldn't budge. Finally, after several firm pokes he made a move . . . the wrong way. Instead of flying forward, he fluttered backward inside the two window panes. Now he was trapped.

What a pitiful sight. A little bird bouncing inside the glass. I had no choice. I stuck my fingers in the opening, grabbed a few feathers, and jerked him out. I'm sure he didn't appreciate the yank, but at least he was free. And when he got back to his nest, did he ever have a story to tell.

"I had a horrible day, Martha. I got stuck in this huge room with a fake exit. They made it look like a hole, but it wasn't. Then they tried to crush me with this moving ledge. But it stopped just before it reached the top. The big, ugly one came after me with a stick. Just when he was about to spear me I made a move for it. I dodged him but fell into their trap—a narrow room with invisible walls. How cruel. I could see them pointing at me. I'm sure they were hungry. Then the ugly one came after me again, this time with his fingers. He was going for my neck. I outfoxed him, though. Just when he pulled me out, I kicked loose and put it in turbocharge and escaped. It's a good thing I did or they would have had hummingburgers for dinner."

I was being kind. The bird thought I was cruel. If only the little bird had known that I had come to help. If only the little fellow had known that I was on his side. If only he had understood that the moving ledge and stick were for his protection.

If only he knew . . .

Now, I may be overdoing it with the hummingbird, but I'm not overdoing it with the point. Daily, God's extended aid is misinterpreted as intended hurt. We complain of closed windows, not noticing the huge open doors. We panic as the ledge rises, oblivious to the exit below. We dodge the stick that guides and avoid the fingers that liberate.

"If only you knew . . ." were my words to the bird.

"If only you knew . . ." are God's words to us.[1]

No lectures. No speeches. No homilies on how far he has come to help. No finger-pointing at our past. None of that. Just an appeal. An appeal for trust. "If only you knew . . ."

"If only you knew that I came to help and not condemn. If only you knew that tomorrow will be better than today. If only you knew the gift I have brought: eternal life. If only you knew I want you safely home."

If only you knew.

What wistful words to come from the lips of God. How kind that he would let us hear them. How crucial that we pause to hear them. If only we knew to trust. Trust that God is in our corner. Trust that God wants what is best. Trust that he really means it when he says, "I have good plans for you, not plans to hurt you. I will give you hope and a good future" (Jer. 29:11).

If only we could learn to trust him.

But how hard it is. We quiver like the bird on the ledge, ducking the hand that comes to help. We forget that he is the pilot and we are his passenger.

We accuse, falsely. We reject, naively.

If only we knew.

When he washed the disciples' feet, he was washing ours; when he calmed their storms, he was calming yours; when he forgave Peter, he was forgiving all the penitent. If only we knew.

He still sends pigeons to convince the lost and music to inspire the dance.

He still makes our storms his path, our graves his proof, and our souls his passion.

He hasn't changed.

He trims branches so we can bear fruit;

    he calls the sheep that we might be safe;

        he hears the prayers of crooks so we might go home.

His thunder is still gentle.

And his gentleness still thunders.

If only you knew "the free gift of God and who it is that is asking you . . ."

The gift and the Giver. If you know them, you know all you need.

Notes

Chapter 2   The Hound of Heaven

1. Francis Thompson, *Poetical Works of Francis Thompson* (New York: Oxford University Press, 1969), 89–94.

2. Ibid.

3. Fred Craddock, *Overhearing the Gospel* (Nashville: Abingdon, 1978), 105–8.

4. Ibid.

5. Frederick Buechner, *The Alphabet of Grace* (New York: HarperCollins, 1970), 43–44.

Chapter 4   Miracle at Midnight

1. They entered the boat at early evening (John 6:16); this probably means around 6:00 P.M. Jesus came to them between 3:00 and 6:00 A.M. (Matt. 14:25).

2. See Deuteronomy 1:2.

Chapter 8   Lessons from the Garden

1. William Barclay, *The Gospel of John*, vol. 2 (Philadelphia: Westminster Press, 1975), 222.

Chapter 9   What to Do with Birthdays

1. This comment and many of the other quips shared here are excerpted from *A Spread of Over 40s Jokes*, edited by Helen Exley and published by Exley Publications, Ltd., Mount Kisco, New York 1992.

2. This story was also told by Gary Thomas in "Wise Christians Clip Obituaries," *Christianity Today*, 3 Oct. 1994, 24–27.

Chapter 11   A Different Kind of Hero

1. This Associated Press story appeared in the insert accompanying the audio tape, "Stones in the Road" by Mary Chapin Carpenter, 1994, Sony Music Entertainment, Inc., New York. Mary Chapin Carpenter wrote a song, "John Doe No. 24," after she read this story in the newspaper.

Chapter 13   A Cinderella Story

1. John R. W. Stott, *The Cross of Christ* (Downers Grove, Ill.: InterVarsity Press, 1986), 88.

Chapter 14   The Bad News Preacher

1. This day is outlined and developed in Max Lucado, *In the Eye of the Storm: A Day in the Life of Jesus* (Dallas: Word, 1991).

Chapter 16   Inside Out

1. Adapted from John Phillips, *Exploring the Gospels: John* (Neptune, N.J.: Loizeaux Brother, 1989), 64–65.

Chapter 22   God's Been Known to Niggle

1. Beth Arnold, "The Need to Niggle," *American Way*, 1 June 1991, 44.

Chapter 24   The Winsomeness of Holiness

1. A. Gordon Nasby, ed., *1041 Sermon Illustrations, Ideas and Expositions* (Grand Rapids: Baker, 1976), 186.

Chapter 27   Peter, Me, and Wile E. Coyote
1. James F. Colianni, *The Book of Pulpit Humor* (Ventnor, N.J.: Voicings Publications, 1992), 128.

Chapter 28   Ready for Home
1. Annie Dillard, *Teaching a Stone to Talk* (New York: HarperCollins, 1988), 43.
2. Ibid.
3. Gary Thomas, "Wise Christians Clip Obituaries," *Christianity Today*, 3 October 1994, 24–27.

Chapter 30   If Only You Knew
1. See John 4:10.

Discussion Guide

Prepared by Steve Halliday

How to Use This Discussion Guide

Each of these short studies is designed not only to help you digest and apply the ideas developed in *A Gentle Thunder*, but also to point you back to Scripture as the wellspring of those ideas.

The first section of each study, "Echoes of Thunder," excerpts portions of each chapter and supplies questions for group discussion. The second section, "Flashes of Lightning," helps you dig a little deeper into Scripture's perspective on the topic under discussion.

His Voice, Our Choice

Echoes of Thunder

1. "How far do you want God to go in getting your attention? If God has to choose between your eternal safety and your earthly comfort, which do you hope he chooses?"
   A. Answer Max's two questions above.
   B. How far have you seen God go in getting others' attention?

2. "For all its peculiarities and unevenness, the Bible has a simple story. God made man. Man rejected God. God won't give up until he wins him back."
   A. What does Max mean by the Bible's "peculiarities and unevenness"?
   B. Name several biblical examples of what Max is describing here.

3. "God is as creative as he is relentless. The same hand that sent manna to Israel sent Uzzah to his death. The same hand that set the children free from Egypt also sent them captive to Babylon. Both kind and stern. Tender and tough."
   A. How could God be both kind and stern?
   B. In what ways has God been "creative" in your own life? How have you seen both his kindness and his toughness?

4. "God will whisper. He will shout. He will touch and tug. He will take away our burdens; he'll even take away our blessings. If there are a thousand steps between us and him, he will take all but one. But he will leave the final one for us. The choice is ours."
   A. How does it make you feel to know that God will go to such extremes to retrieve us? Explain.
   B. What is this "final choice" Max writes about? What choice have you made? Explain.

Flashes of Lightning

1. Read Psalm 81:6–16.
   A. How does this passage demonstrate both the kindness and the toughness of God? What events does this psalm describe?
   B. What is the Lord's chief desire for us, according to this psalm (see especially verses 10, 13–14, 16)?

2. Read Romans 11:22.
   A. What two traits is Paul contrasting in this verse?
   B. What example does Paul use to illustrate what he says in this verse?

3. Read John 5:6; 9:35; 11:25–26.
   A. What is Jesus doing in each of these texts? Why is he doing this?
   B. What choice would Jesus ask you to make if he were to speak to you today, face-to-face?

Chapter 1   The Author of Life

Echoes of Thunder

1. "The Author starts each life story, but each life will write his or her own ending."
   A. What does Max mean in his statement above?
   B. What kind of "ending" are you writing for your own story?

2. "Love is only love if chosen."
   A. Do you agree with this statement? Why or why not?
   B. Is love merely a choice, or is it more than that? Explain.

3. "Emmanuel would stand at the crossroads of life and death and make a choice."
   A. What choice did Emmanuel have to make? How did this affect you personally?
   B. How did Emmanuel make the choice he made? What gave him the strength to do so?

Flashes of Lightning

1. Read Deuteronomy 30:15–20.
   A. What choice was set before the nation of Israel? How is this choice similar to the one before us? How is it different?
   B. What choice did the nation finally make? What were the results? Can this be an example for us? Explain.

2. Read 1 John 4:7–21.
   A. What do you learn about love in this passage? Is it chosen? How can you tell?
   B. What is the primary example of love described in this passage (v. 10)? Was this love chosen? Explain.

3. Read Matthew 4:1–11; Luke 22:39–44.
   A. What choice did Emmanuel have to make in the Matthew passage? How did he make this choice?
   B. What choice did Emmanuel have to make in the Luke passage? How did he make this choice?
   C. How can we follow Emmanuel's example in the choices we make?

Chapter 2   The Hound of Heaven

Echoes of Thunder

1. "The rest of the world is occupied with Germany and Hitler. Every headline is reporting the actions of Roosevelt and Churchill. The globe is locked in a battle for freedom . . . and the Father is in the Pacific sending a missionary pigeon to save a soul."
   A. What does this incident teach us about God? How wide is his field of view?
   B. What kinds of "missionary pigeons" has God sent into your own life or into the lives of loved ones? Describe them.

2. "If anyone is in Christ, it is because Christ has called him."
   A. Do you agree with this statement? Why or why not?
   B. How did Christ call you?

3. "It isn't the circumstance that matters; it is God in the circumstance. It isn't the words; it is God speaking them."
   A. What do you think Max means by this statement? What point is he trying to make?
   B. Give an example from your own life of the difference between circumstances and God in those circumstances.

4. "The cradle and the cross were as common as grass. What made them holy was the One laid upon them."
   A. In what way were the cradle and the cross made "holy"? What does it mean that they were made holy?
   B. What makes common things holy today? What is being made holy in your own experience?

Flashes of Lightning

1. Read John 4:4.
   A. How is the story of the Samaritan woman like the one about the American flyers in World War II? What similarities do you see?

  B. Why do you think Jesus "had" to go through Samaria?

2. Read John 6:37–40, 44–45.
  A. According to these verses, how do people come to Christ?
  B. What promise does Jesus make in verses 39–40? Is this a promise you can claim? Explain.

3. Read Ephesians 4:22–24.
  A. What are we commanded to do in this passage? Why?
  B. How does "holiness" work its way out into everyday living? Name several examples.

Chapter 3   Come and See

Echoes of Thunder

  1. "Is the life of the young Nazarene carpenter really worth considering?"
    A. Answer Max's question above, then give a reason for your answer.
    B. What about the "life of the young Nazarene carpenter" is most worth considering, in your opinion? Why?

  2. "Come and see the pierced hand of God touch the most common heart, wipe the tear from the wrinkled face, and forgive the ugliest sin."
    A. Does the "pierced hand of God" continue to do these things today? If so, how?
    B. Give examples from your own life of how Christ has done the three things listed in Max's statement above.

  3. "Come and see. He avoids no seeker. He ignores no probe. He fears no search. Come and see."
    A. Why would Jesus "avoid no seeker, ignore no probe, or fear no search"? What enabled him to live this way?
    B. Do you invite people to "come and see" Jesus today? Explain.

Flashes of Lightning

  1. Read Hebrews 12:3.
    A. Who are we asked to "consider" in this verse? What reason is given?
    B. In what way do you "consider" him? How does this help your everyday life?

2. Read Isaiah 42:1–4.
   A. List the activities of the coming Messiah as described in this passage.
   B. How do Jesus' activities compare to this list?

3. Read John 1:43–46.
   A. What happens in this passage? Describe it.
   B. What "evangelistic method" does Philip use in this passage? Can you use this method? Why or why not?

Chapter 4   Miracle at Midnight

Echoes of Thunder

1. "They did exactly what Jesus said, and look what it got them! A night on a storm-tossed sea with their Master somewhere on the shore."
   A. How do you think the disciples were feeling at this point? Why?
   B. Have you ever felt like this? If so, describe the circumstances.

2. "It's one thing to suffer for doing wrong. Something else entirely to suffer for doing right. But it happens."
   A. How does suffering for doing something wrong differ from suffering from doing right? They're both suffering, aren't they?
   B. If you have ever suffered for doing right, describe the circumstances.

3. "God was more concerned that they arrive *prepared* than that they arrive *soon*."
   A. What did it mean in this case that the disciples arrive "prepared"?
   B. In what way is this a good summary of God's work in our own lives?

4. "There are certain passions learned only by pain. And there are times when God, knowing that, allows us to endure the pain for the sake of the song."
   A. What kind of "passions" are learned only by pain? Why is pain the best teacher?
   B. Describe an instance in your own life when God allowed you to endure pain "for the sake of the song."

5. "We have our share of feasts, but we also have our share of baloney sandwiches. And to have the first we must endure the second."

A. Do you agree with this statement? Why or why not?

B. What kind of "feasts" have you enjoyed? Did they usually follow "baloney sandwiches"? Explain.

Flashes of Lightning

1. Read John 6:16–21.
    A. How was this experience like those we sometimes have?
    B. How did the disciples react when they saw Jesus? Did they know it was Jesus right away? What did they do when they made the discovery?

2. Read 1 Peter 4:15–16.
    A. What kinds of suffering does this passage describe?
    B. What kind of suffering should not make us ashamed? Why?

3. Read Acts 14:21–22.
    A. What did Paul and Barnabas do in Lystra, Iconium and Antioch? How did they do this?
    B. What did they tell the disciples in verse 22? How could this actually be an encouragement?

Chapter 5   The Secret of Forgiveness

Echoes of Thunder

1. "Logic says: 'She doesn't deserve it.' Jesus says: 'You're right, but you don't either.'"
    A. Why does logic say, "She doesn't deserve it"? Have you ever thought this way? If so, explain.
    B. Does Jesus refute this logic? How does he respond to it? Why is this important?

2. "We cannot cleanse our own filth. We cannot remove our own sin. Our feet must be in his hands."
    A. Why cannot we cleanse our own filth?
    B. In what sense today must our "feet . . . be in his hands"?

3. "Jesus is assuming the role of the servant. He will wash the grimiest part of your life. If you let him."
    A. Do you think Jesus will still assume the role of the servant today? Explain.
    B. How does Jesus "wash the grimiest" part of our life? What is necessary for this to happen?

4. "We will never be cleansed until we confess we are dirty."
   A. Why is it necessary to confess we are "dirty"? What does this entail?
   B. Have you made such a confession? Explain.

5. "God will never call you to do what he hasn't already done."
   A. Do you agree with this statement? Why or why not?
   B. What is the hardest thing God has called you to do? How do you know he called you to do it? How can you accomplish it?

Flashes of Lightning

1. Read John 13:3–5,12–17.
   A. What reason is given in verse 3 for what Jesus did? How is this significant?
   B. What lesson did Jesus want his disciples to learn in verses 12–17? What lesson is here for us?

2. Read 1 John 1:8–10.
   A. How does this text say we sometimes deceive ourselves?
   B. How can we be forgiven for our sins?
   C. In what way do some people call God a liar?

3. Read 2 Thessalonians 2:13–17.
   A. According to verse 13, how are we saved?
   B. What is the result of this in verse 14?
   C. What is Paul's prayer in verses 16–17? How is this connected to verses 13–15?

Chapter 6   The Bread of Life

Echoes of Thunder

1. "What bread is to hunger, Jesus claims to be for the soul."
   A. What does bread do for hunger?
   B. What does Jesus claim to do for our soul? In what way does Jesus want us to see him like bread?

2. "Jesus adapts himself to meet our need."
   A. How does Jesus adapt himself to meet our need?
   B. In what ways has Jesus adapted himself to meet your need?

3. "Jesus experienced each part of the process of making bread: the growing, the pounding, the firing."
   A. Describe the "growing, the pounding, and the firing" that Jesus went through.
   B. Why was it important for Jesus to go through all these steps? Why not bypass some or all of them?

4. "We can't force people to eat the bread, but we can make sure they have it. Yet, for some reason we are reluctant to do so. It's much easier to stay in the bakery than get into the truck."
   A. How can we make sure people have this "bread"? Have you made sure they had it? Explain.
   B. Why do we find it easier to stay in the bakery? How can we motivate ourselves to get into the truck?

5. "I don't know what is more incredible: that God packages the bread of life in the wrapper of a country carpenter or that he gives us the keys to the delivery truck."
   A. Which of these two facts is more incredible to you? Why?
   B. What are you doing with the keys to the delivery truck? Explain.

Flashes of Lightning

1. Read John 6:35–36.
   A. What claim did Jesus make in verse 35?
   B. What is one possible reaction to Jesus' claim (verse 36)?

2. Read Isaiah 55:1–3.
   A. What invitation is given here? How is it similar to what Jesus said in John 6?
   B. How would you answer the question in verse 2?
   C. What is promised in verses 2b–3?

3. Read Luke 24:25–26.
   A. To whom was Jesus speaking in this verse? Why do you think he took this tone with them?
   B. What did Jesus explain in verse 26? How does this help to explain what happened at Calvary?

Chapter 7   For Longer Than Forever

Echoes of Thunder

1. "We are a gnat on the tail of one elephant in a galaxy of Africas, and yet we demand that God finds us a parking place when we ask."
   A. What point is Max driving at in the statement above?
   B. Have you ever found yourself making such a demand? If so, describe the circumstances. How do you feel about it now?

2. "Our evil cannot diminish God's love. Our goodness cannot increase it. Our faith does not earn it any more than our stupidity jeopardizes it."
   A. Why can't our evil diminish God's love? Why can't our goodness increase it?
   B. If our faith doesn't "earn" God's love, how can we receive it? Why can't our stupidity jeopardize that love?

3. "God has no cousins, only children."
   A. Explain the statement above. What does it mean?
   B. Why doesn't God have any cousins, only children? What kind of people might be tempted to think they're God's cousins?

4. "Nothing can separate us from the love of Christ . . . but how difficult it is for some to embrace this truth."
   A. Why is it sometimes difficult for us to embrace the fact that nothing can separate us from the love of Christ?
   B. How do you respond to this truth personally? How do you remind yourself of it? Does it affect the way you live? Explain.

Flashes of Lightning

1. Read John 13:1
   A. What time was it, according to this verse? How did Jesus know this?
   B. What was Jesus about to show his disciples? How would he show them this?

2. Read Psalm 136.
   A. What refrain is repeated multiple times in this psalm?
   B. Why is this so important? What lesson is being taught?

3. Read Romans 8:38–39.
   A. What promise is given in this passage?
   B. How does God love us, according to this passage? Why is this crucial?

Chapter 8   Lessons from the Garden

Echoes of Thunder

1. "Were the moment not so solemn it would be comic. These are the best soldiers with Satan's finest plan, yet one word from Jesus and they fall down!"
   A. In what way is this moment solemn? In what way might it be comic?
   B. What do you think might have been running through Satan's mind at this time? What might Judas have been thinking?

2. "Don't miss the symbolism here: When Jesus speaks, Satan falls."
   A. In what way is this statement a spiritual principle?
   B. Have you ever seen this principle at work in the life of your family or church? If so, explain.

3. "When Jesus says he will keep you safe, he means it. Hell will have to get through him to get to you."
   A. How does this statement make you feel? Why?
   B. In what ways has Jesus kept you safe thus far?

4. "I'll show you the way; you fill in the blanks:
   "Precious Father, I praise your name. You have reclaimed so much in my life. I was lost, and you found me. I was confused, and you guided me. I had nothing to offer but still you loved me.
   "I confess that I still need help. I have a part of my life that needs your touch. Satan is battling for a garden in my heart. Don't let him win. Drive him out. He is a liar and has been since the beginning. Please defeat him. I'll give you the glory.
   "Here is the area where I need your strength _____."

Flashes of Lightning

1. Read John 18:1–9.
   A. Who appears to be in charge of this event? Why do you say this?
   B. In what way were the events of the garden a fulfillment of prophecy (see especially verse 9)?

2. Read Ephesians 6:10–13.
  A. What are we instructed to do in verses 10 and 11? What is the reason for this command?
  B. What kind of struggle are we involved in (verse 12)? How should this change our strategies?

3. Read 2 Timothy 4:16–18.
  A. What had happened to Paul?
  B. Who alone stood with Paul? Why did he stand with him?
  C. What promise is made in verse 18?

Chapter 9   What to Do with Birthdays

Echoes of Thunder

1. "When you are young you make a lot of faces in the mirror. When you are old the mirror gets even."
  A. Is your own mirror getting even with you?
  B. How do you think most people feel about getting older? When does it finally start to dawn on them that one day they'll have to face death?

2. "Is death when we go to sleep? Or is death when we finally wake up?"
  A. How would you answer Max's question above?
  B. How do you think most of your friends view death?

3. "For God, death is no tragedy. In God's economy the termination of the body is the beginning of life."
  A. Why does God view death differently than we do?
  B. In what way is the termination of the body the beginning of life? What biblical support can you cite for this view?

4. "By calling us home, God is doing what any father would do. He is providing a better place to rest."
  A. Why would heaven be a better place to rest than where we are now?
  B. Where do you expect to be resting after your time on earth is finished? Explain.

5. "I've often thought it curious how few people Jesus raised from the dead. Could it be that once someone is there, the last place they want to return to is here?"
   A. What do you think about Max's question? How would you respond?
   B. Suppose you were to die tonight. Would you want to be called back to live on earth in four days? Explain.

Flashes of Lightning

1. Read John 14:1–3.
   A. What command does Jesus give in verse 1? What reason does he give for following the command?
   B. What promise does Jesus give us in verses 2–3?

2. Read Luke 12:37–38.
   A. To what does Jesus liken his return in this passage?
   B. What does he promise us?

3. Read Isaiah 57:1–2 and Psalm 116:15.
   A. Why does God sometimes take good people home "early," according to Isaiah? What benefit do they receive?
   B. How does God view the death of his children, according to the psalmist? How can he view it this way?

Chapter 10   Music for the Dance

Echoes of Thunder

1. "We Christians are prone to follow the book while ignoring the music."
   A. What does Max mean by this statement?
   B. Is this an error you are prone to make? Why or why not?

2. "Of the three persons of the Godhead, the Holy Spirit is the one we understand the least."
   A. Would you agree with this statement? Why or why not?
   B. How well do you think you understand the Holy Spirit? Where do you get your information?

3. "Emotion without knowledge is as dangerous as knowledge without emotion. God seeks a balance."
   A. Why is emotion without knowledge dangerous? Why is knowledge without emotion dangerous?

B. How can you practically balance emotion with knowledge?

Flashes of Lightning

1. Read John 16:7–15; 14:17; 4:24.
   A. What do you learn about the Spirit in John 16:7–15?
   B. What do you learn about the Spirit in John 14:17?
   C. What do you learn about the Spirit's work in John 4:24?

2. Read Romans 8:10–12.
   A. What work of the Spirit is described in verse 11?
   B. Because this is true, to what are we obligated (verse 12)?

3. Read Acts 5:3–4; Ephesians 4:30; Hebrews 10:29.
   A. How does the Acts passage demonstrate that the Holy Spirit is a person?
   B. How does the Ephesians passage demonstrate that the Holy Spirit is a person?
   C. How does Hebrews 10:29 demonstrate that the Holy Spirit is a person?

Chapter 11   A Different Kind of Hero

Echoes of Thunder

1. "Aren't we glad Christ didn't call himself the Good Cowboy?"
   A. What's the main difference between a shepherd and a cowboy?
   B. Are you glad Christ didn't call himself the Good Cowboy? Explain.

2. "We don't need a cowboy to herd us; we need a shepherd to care for us and to guide us."
   A. Do you know of anyone who sees God as a cowboy rather than a shepherd? If so, describe him or her.
   B. Have you ever felt like you were being "herded" rather than "shepherded" by someone in authority? If so, what was the difference? How did you feel about it?

3. "He guides, feeds, and anoints. And Word has it that he won't quit until we reach the homeland."
   A. How does Jesus guide us today? How does he feed us? How does he anoint us?
   B. How do you know "he won't quit until we reach the homeland"? What is this homeland?

Flashes of Lightning

1. Read John 10:1–16.
    A. What lessons was Jesus trying to give his disciples in verses 1–5? Did they understand?
    B. How did Jesus make clear the lesson in verses 7–16?

2. Read Psalm 23:1–4; 79:13; 80:1; 95:7; 100:3.
    A. How did Jesus build on all these passages in his speech of John 10?
    B. What implication was Jesus making?

3. Read 1 Peter 2:25; Hebrews 13:20.
    A. How does Peter picture the Lord?
    B. How does the writer of Hebrews picture the Lord?

Chapter 12   Held by His Hands

Echoes of Thunder

1. "I can't tell you how many times I've expected to hit the bottom only to find myself suspended in midair, secured by a pair of pierced hands."
    A. If you have ever had an experience such as the one Max mentions above, describe it.
    B. How does it give us confidence to know that we have such a God?

2. "Though you can't see your guide, you know him. You know he is strong. You know he is able to keep you from falling."
    A. How can you know your guide if you can't see him?
    B. How do you know God is able to keep you from falling?

3. "You are only a few more steps from the top. So whatever you do, don't quit. Though your falls are great, his strength is greater. You *will* make it."
    A. If you have ever known someone who was tempted to quit just a few steps from the top, describe what happened.
    B. What would tempt you to quit just a few steps from the top? How would you overcome these temptations?

Flashes of Lightning

1. Read John 10:28–30.
    A. What does Jesus say he does in verse 28? What does he say no one can do?

B. How does what Jesus says in verses 29-30 back up what he said in verse 28?

2. Read Jude 24–25.
    A. What is promised in verse 24?
    B. What should be our response (verse 25)?

3. Read Philippians 1:6.
    A. Who began "a good work" in you?
    B. What else will he do? When will this job be finished?

Chapter 13   A Cinderella Story

Echoes of Thunder

1. "God between two thieves. Exactly the place he wants to be."
    A. Why would God want to be between two thieves?
    B. In what way does God still want to be between two thieves?

2. "Sin is not an unfortunate slip or a regrettable act; it is a posture of defiance against a holy God."
    A. How would the people you work with define sin? How would your neighbors define it?
    B. In what way is every sin an act of defiance against a holy God?

3. "The one with no sin becomes sin-filled. The one sin-filled becomes sinless. It's eternity's most bizarre exchange."
    A. Why would Max call this "eternity's most bizarre exchange"? When did this exchange take place?
    B. Can we completely understand this exchange? Explain. What mystery might still remain?

4. "Jesus gave more than a kiss—he gave his beauty. He paid more than a visit—he paid for our mistakes. He took more than a minute—he took away our sin."
    A. In what ways was Jesus' act similar to that of the woman who played Cinderella? In what ways was it different?
    B. How did Jesus pay for our mistakes? How did he take away our sin? Why could only he do this?

Flashes of Lightning

1. Read Luke 23:39–43.
    A. How were the two criminals' responses different from one another?

B. What request did one of the criminals make? How was it answered?

2. Read Psalm 51:1–4.
   A. What request did David make in verses 1–2?
   B. What confession did David make in verses 3–4? Why is verse 4 especially important?

3. Read 2 Corinthians 5:19, 21.
   A. What is "the message of reconciliation"? Who bears it?
   B. What exchange is detailed in verse 21? In what way is this the gospel in brief?

4. Read Isaiah 53:4–6.
   A. Who is being described in verses 4-5? What did he do?
   B. How are we described in verse 6? How is this connected to verses 4-5?

Chapter 14   The Bad News Preacher

Echoes of Thunder

1. "God's faithfulness has never depended on the faithfulness of his children. He is faithful even when we aren't."
   A. Why doesn't God's faithfulness depend on our own faithfulness?
   B. Describe a time in your life when this truth was highlighted.

2. "Though the answer to prayer is standing next to him, he doesn't even pray."
   A. Why do you think the disciples failed to ask Jesus to do something about their situation?
   B. In what way are we often like the disciples?

3. "I simply think God is greater than our weakness. In fact, I think it is our weakness that reveals how great God is."
   A. How does our weakness reveal how great God is?
   B. How has God shown his greatness through your own weakness?

4. "If Jesus would have acted according to the faith of his disciples, the multitudes would have gone unfed. But he didn't, and he doesn't. God is true to us even when we forget him."
   A. Why do you think God sometimes chooses to act according to our faith and sometimes not?

B. Describe some times in your own life when God was true to you even when you perhaps forgot him.

Flashes of Lightning

1. Read John 6:5–13.
   A. What question did Jesus ask in verse 5? Why did he ask this according to verse 6?
   B. What was the main lesson of verses 7–13?

2. Read 2 Corinthians 12:9–10.
   A. What claim did God make in verse 9?
   B. How did Paul respond to this claim in verse 10?

3. Read 2 Timothy 2:13.
   A. What happens when we are "faithless," according to this verse?
   B. Why does this happen? What does this mean?

Chapter 15   The Final Witness

Echoes of Thunder

1. "'The dead hear only the voice of God . . . ,' said Lazarus . . . 'I heard the voice of God.'"
   A. If a man is dead, how can he hear anything?
   B. How did Lazarus know it was the voice of God he heard?
   C. In what way do "dead men" still hear the voice of God today?

2. "Jesus said, 'I will do for him what I did for them. I'll give him joy, strength, healing, sight, safety, nourishment, new life.'"
   A. Does Jesus still give us joy, strength, healing, sight, safety, nourishment, and new life today? If so, how?
   B. Which of the gifts listed above means the most to you? Explain your choice.

3. "The Master has offered to do for you what he did for them. He will bring wine to your table, sight to your eyes, strength for your step and, most of all, power over your grave. He will do for you what he did for them. The Judge has given his blessing. The rest is up to you."
   A. Name some Scripture verses where God offers you the things listed above.
   B. What is the choice you must make? What choice have you made? Why did you make this choice?

Flashes of Lightning

1. Read John 20:29–31.
   A. Who is especially blessed, according to verse 29? Why?
   B. What was the purpose of writing down Jesus' miracles? Have they had this intended effect on you? Why or why not?

2. Read Luke 3:21–22.
   A. What happened as described in this text?
   B. Why is this so crucial to everything that happens later?

3. Read Ephesians 2:1–5.
   A. How could we be described in our pre-Christian days, according to verses 1–3?
   B. How was our status changed as described in verses 4–5? What prompted this change in status?

Chapter 16   Inside Out

Echoes of Thunder

1. "A walking cat is still a cat. The same is true with people."
   A. What does Max mean by the statement above?
   B. Does this mean that not even God can change our basic natures? Explain.

2. "According to the Bible, there is one thing we cannot change—our sinful state."
   A. Why can't we change our sinful state on our own?
   B. Does this mean we are left to deal with this sinful state throughout our lives? Explain.

3. "It is through God's pain that we are born. It's not our struggle, but God's. It's not our blood shed, but his."
   A. How is God "pained" through our spiritual birth?
   B. In what way is our salvation God's struggle? Whose blood was shed to gain our salvation? How does this "work"?

4. "God is as polite as he is passionate. He never forces his way in. The choice is theirs."
   A. Do you agree with this statement? Why or why not?
   B. Does God ever intrude into our lives without asking? What about in the life of Saul (who became the apostle Paul) described in Acts 9:1–17?

5. "The first time you had no choice about being born; this time you do."
    A. What choice have you made about being born a second time?
    B. What prompted you to make this choice?

Flashes of Lightning

1. Read John 3:3–8,14–18.
    A. What is the only way to enter the kingdom of God, according to this passage? What does this mean?
    B. What illustration does Jesus give in verses 14–18? How does this illustration help explain what he was to do?

2. Read 2 Corinthians 6:1–2.
    A. What does it mean to "receive God's grace in vain"? How is this possible?
    B. When is the best time to be saved, according to verse 2?

3. Read Galatians 3:13-14.
    A. How did Christ redeem us from the curse? What does it mean to be redeemed from the curse?
    B. Why did he redeem us, according to verse 14?

Chapter 17 The Yay-Yuck Man

Echoes of Thunder

1. "Now Bob could be any color, any time, and please every person."
    A. If you were asked to pick one word to describe Bob, what would it be? Why would you pick this word?
    B. Why are we sometimes tempted to act like Bob?

2. "Everyone liked him because everyone thought he was just like them."
    A. Why do we like others who seem just like us?
    B. What is the huge trap concealed in this kind of attitude?

3. "'It's not their approval I seek,' said the man."
    A. Who does this man represent? Why do you think so?
    B. Whose approval do you seek? Why?

4. "'I am here to show people they don't have to please people,' the man said. 'I am here to tell the truth.'"
    A. Have you ever felt as if you had to please people? If so, why did you feel this way?

B. What is the best way of reminding ourselves we don't have to please people?

Flashes of Lightning

1. Read John 8:39–47.
    A. What truth did Jesus tell the Pharisees? How did they respond?
    B. Why couldn't the Pharisees believe Jesus, according to verse 47?

2. Read Galatians 4:16–18.
    A. What question did Paul ask in verse 16? How might this be possible?
    B. Why did Paul tell them the truth, according to verses 17–18?

3. Read Galatians 1:10.
    A. What question did Paul ask here?
    B. What answer does he give to his own question? What does this imply for us?

Chapter 18   Calamities of the Common Scale

Echoes of Thunder

1. "She simply assessed the problem and gave it to Christ."
    A. Why is it important to assess a problem? How do you assess problems in your own life?
    B. What does it mean to "give a problem to Christ"? How do you do this in a practical sense?

2. "What causes us to think of prayer as the last option rather than the first?"
    A. How would you answer Max's question?
    B. How quickly do you normally think of prayer when a problem arises? Are you satisfied with this? Why or why not?

3. "My daughters' maturity and mobility are good and necessary, but I hope they never get to the point where they are too grown up to call their daddy."
    A. In what way might this statement be a reflection of God's thoughts about us?
    B. Have you ever known anyone who thought they were "too grown up" for God? If so, explain.

4. "Note, the water became wine *after* they had they obeyed, not before."
   A. Why is it significant that the water became wine after the men had obeyed?
   B. How is this applicable to us today?

Flashes of Lightning

1. Read John 2:1–11.
   A. What instruction did Mary give in verse 5? Why do you think she did this?
   B. What was the purpose of this demonstration, according to verse 11? What was the result?

2. Read Psalm 50:15–21.
   A. What are we instructed to do in verse 15? What does God promise to do? How are we to respond?
   B. To whom is this promise directed? How do verses 16–21 make this clear?

3. Read 1 Samuel 15:22–23a.
   A. What question is asked in verse 22a? What response is given in 22b?
   B. To what is disobedience compared in verse 23? How is this significant?

Chapter 19   Your Place in God's Band

Echoes of Thunder

1. "Marthas are the Energizer bunnies of the church. They keep going and going and going."
   A. Are you more like a Martha, a Mary, or a Lazarus? Explain.
   B. Describe some of the Marthas in your church.

2. "Marys are gifted with praise. They don't just sing; they worship. They don't simply attend church; they go to offer praise. They don't just talk about Christ; they radiate Christ."
   A. What's the difference between mere singing and worship? Between attending church and offering praise? Between talking about Christ and radiating Christ?
   B. Describe some of the Marys in your church.

3. "Marys need to remember that service is worship. Marthas need to remember that worship is service. And Lazarus? He needs to remember that not everyone can play the trumpet."
   A. How can service be worship? How can worship be service?
   B. Can you "play the trumpet"? Why or why not? If you can't, who in your acquaintance can? Explain.

4. "Are you near Christ, but far from his heart? Are you at the dinner with a sour soul? Are you always criticizing the gifts of others, yet seldom, if ever, giving your own? Are you benefiting from the church while never giving to it? Do others give sacrificially while you give miserly? Are you a Judas?"
   A. How would you answer each of the six questions listed above?
   B. Are you satisfied with how you're fitting in with God's band? Why or why not?

Flashes of Lightning

1. Read John 12:1–6.
   A. What did Mary do in this passage? Why did she do it?
   B. How did Judas respond? Why did he respond like this?
   C. What lesson is intended for us?

2. Read Luke 10:38–42.
   A. What's was Martha's complaint? What prompted it?
   B. How did Jesus respond? What principle did he lay down?

3. Read Romans 12:4–8.
   A. What does this passage teach us about unity? What does it teach us about diversity?
   B. What does it teach us about the relationship of the two?

Chapter 20   Extravagant Love

Echoes of Thunder

1. "Jesus reduces the number of life's struggles to two. We either strive for food that rots or food that lasts."
   A. How do you strive for food that rots? What kind of food is this?
   B. How do you strive for food that lasts? What kind of food is this?

2. "I know he said he would give it but, honestly now, how do we pay for this bread? How do we earn this meal? How long do we have to stand in the cafeteria line to get the eternal food?"
   A. Do you ever find yourself thinking along the lines described above? If so, explain.
   B. Why are we so often tempted to try to pay back grace? Why is this impossible?

3. "Have you ever considered what an insult it is to God when we try to pay him for his goodness?"
   A. Answer Max's question above.
   B. Why is this such an insult?

4. "Apart from Christ you aren't holy. So how may we go to heaven? Only believe."
   A. Why aren't we holy apart from Christ?
   B. How does Christ make us holy? Has he made you holy? Explain.

Flashes of Lightning

1. Read John 6:26–29.
   A. What command does Jesus give in verse 27?
   B. How do his hearers respond in verse 28?
   C. What reply does Jesus give in verse 29? What is unusual about this response?

2. Read Hebrews 12:14–17.
   A. What command are we given in verse 14? What warning is given?
   B. What practical outworking of this command is described in verses 15–17? How are these verses related to verse 14?

3. Read Acts 17:24–31.
   A. What does Paul tell his hearers about God in verse 25? Why is this significant?
   B. What is God's desire as expressed in verse 27?
   C. What does God demand in verse 30?
   D. What does he warn in verse 31?

Chapter 21   God's Fondest Dream

Echoes of Thunder

1. "Suspicion and distrust often lurk at God's table. Around the table the siblings squabble and the Father sighs."
   A. Why do suspicion and distrust often lurk at God's table?
   B. How have you seen "the siblings squabble"? Why does the Father sigh?

2. "Never in the Bible are we told to create unity. We are simply told to maintain the unity that exists."
   A. Why does the Bible not ask us to create unity?
   B. How are we to maintain unity with one another?

3. "We Christians wouldn't be known for what divides us, but instead we'd be known for what unites us—our common Father."
   A. Do you think we Christians are known for what divides us? Explain your answer.
   B. How could we become known for what unites us? What would we have to do? What would we have to change?

Flashes of Lightning

1. Read John 17:20–23.
   A. What is Jesus' primary request in this passage?
   B. Why does he make this request, according to verse 23?

2. Read Ephesians 4:2–13.
   A. What commands are given in verses 2–3?
   B. What basis for these commands is given in verses 4–11?
   C. What is the purpose of these commands as detailed in verses 12–13?

3. Read 1 John 3:11–18.
   A. What command is given in verse 11?
   B. What negative example is given in verse 12? How is this significant?
   C. How does John make unity a practical matter in verses 13–18?

Chapter 22 God's Been Known to Niggle

Echoes of Thunder

1. "God loves to find anything that impedes our growth. Jesus portrays him as the Good Gardener who cuts and trims the vine."
   A. What things most often impede your growth?
   B. How does God cut and trim the vines in your own life?

2. "You've seen gardeners realign a plant, and you've probably seen God realign a life."
   A. How do gardeners realign a plant? What do they do?
   B. How is God's work like this? What similarities do you see?

3. "You can't force fruit. That's why nowhere in this text does Jesus tell you to go out and bear fruit."
   A. Do you know people who feel as if they must force fruit to appear in their life? Why do you think they feel this way? What could you tell them?
   B. If Jesus doesn't tell us to bear fruit, what does he tell us to do? How do we do this?

4. "Our task? It's clear. Stay close to the vine. As long as we do, we'll be fruitful."
   A. What do you do in order to stay close to the vine? What moves you away from the vine?
   B. When you are close to the vine, what kind of fruit do you produce? What happens when you move away from the vine?

5. "Even now, some of you are hearing the snip-snip-snip of his shears. It hurts. But take heart. You'll be better as a result."
   A. What kind of pruning is needed most in your life right now? Why do you say this?
   B. Does realizing what God is doing in your life help you bear the pain of the pruning? Explain.

Flashes of Lightning

1. Read John 15:1–8.
   A. In what ways is God like a gardener?
   B. In what ways is Jesus like a vine?
   C. In what ways are we like branches?

2. Read Galatians 5:22–23.
   A. What kind of fruit is God most interested in?
   B. Does this fruit characterize you? Why or why not?

3. Read Hebrews 12:11.
   A. What does this verse admit about discipline?
   B. What encouragement does it give us to continue on?

Chapter 23   The Parable of the Sandwich Sign

Echoes of Thunder

1. "You must stand on the side of the road and warn the drivers not to make the left turn."
   A. Who do these men represent in this parable?
   B. What are they required to do? Why?

2. "Hundreds of lives were saved by the three sign holders. Because they did their job, many people were kept from peril."
   A. With which of the three sign holders can you most readily identify? Why?
   B. How do we keep people from peril in our own world?

3. "The first man got sleepy. The second didn't grow tired, but he did grow conceited. The third man was concerned about the message of his sign. It troubled him that his message was so narrow, so dogmatic."
   A. Which of the men's three different problems would be most likely to trouble you? Why?
   B. How would you help someone overcome each of the three problems listed here?

4. "As the first man slept and the second stood and the third altered the message, one car after another plunged into the river."
   A. What was the result of these men's failure to do their job?
   B. What lesson does this parable teach us? Is this a lesson you especially need to hear? Explain.

Flashes of Lightning

1. Read John 1:23.
   A. What was John the Baptist's sole purpose, according to this verse?
   B. How did he fulfill this verse?

2. Read Ezekiel 33:7–9.
   A. What does it mean to be a "watchman"?
   B. What instruction is given in verses 8–9? What warning? Does this apply in any way to us? Why or why not?

3. Read 2 Corinthians 5:19b–20.
   A. To whom is the "message of reconciliation" committed?
   B. How did Paul see his responsibilities to the unsaved? How is this connected to us today?

Chapter 24   The Winsomeness of Holiness

Echoes of Thunder

1. "What mattered was that you get off your duff and get right with God because he's coming and he don't mean maybe."
   A. How do you "get off your duff and get right with God"?
   B. What is a huge incentive for doing this?

2. "You don't have to be like the world to have an impact on the world."
   A. Do you agree with this statement? Why or why not?
   B. What kind of an impact on the world do Christians who look just like the world normally enjoy? Why?

3. "Holiness seeks to be like God."
   A. What does the word "holiness" mean to you?
   B. Why does holiness seek to be like God? What kind of attitudes does this produce in us?

4. "When a person's ways and words are the same, the fusion is explosive. But when a person says one thing and lives another, the result is destructive."
   A. Why is the fusion explosive when a person's ways and words are the same?
   B. Why is the result destructive when a person says one thing and lives another?

5. "To call yourself a child of God is one thing. To be called a child of God by those who watch your life is another thing altogether."
   A. Do you call yourself a child of God? Would others who watch your life agree with you? Explain.
   B. How would non-Christians most likely describe you?

Flashes of Lightning

1. Read Luke 1:76–80.
   A. What role was prophesied for John?
   B. What purpose was he to serve?

2. Read Mark 1:4–8.
   A. What did John do in verse 4? What did he look like (verse 6)?
   B. How did the crowds react in verse 5?
   C. What was his particular message (verse 7–8)?

3. Read 1 Thessalonians 4:11–12 and 1 Peter 2:11–12.
   A. What advice does Paul give to the Thessalonians? Why does he give this advice?
   B. What advice does Peter give in verse 11? What reason does he give in verse 12?

Chapter 25   Look Before You Label

Echoes of Thunder

1. "It's easier to talk about a person than to help a person."
   A. Why is it such a big temptation to talk about others in a negative way?
   B. How can we encourage ourselves to refrain from this sinful habit?

2. "Is that to say religious discussion is wrong? Of course not. Is that to say we should be unconcerned for doctrine or lax in a desire for holiness? Absolutely not."
   A. What kind of religious discussion pleases God? What kind displeases him?
   B. What kind of concern for doctrine and desire for holiness pleases God? What kind displeases him?

3. "The man wasn't a victim of fate; he was a miracle waiting to happen."
   A. How was this man "a miracle waiting to happen"?
   B. Do we ever know ahead of time who is a miracle waiting to happen? What does this fact suggest to you?

4. "What is the work of God? Accepting people. Loving before judging. Caring before condemning."
   A. How can we learn to accept people if this has not been our practice?

B. Would anyone disagree with Max's words above? How could they be just nice-sounding words? How can we put them into practice? What can you do *today*?

Flashes of Lightning

1. Read John 9:1–7.
   A. What reason does Jesus give for the man's blindness in verse 3? Why might this sound cruel to some people? Is it? Explain.
   B. How does this episode demonstrate that Jesus is the light of the world?

2. Read Ephesians 4:15, 25–32.
   A. What does it mean to "speak the truth in love"? How do you do this in practice?
   B. How are verses 25–32 an illustration of verse 15?

3. Read Matthew 7:1–5.
   A. What command does Jesus give us in verse 1? What is the reason for this command in verse 2?
   B. How are verses 3–5 an illustration of Jesus' command in verse 1?

Chapter 26   Looking for the Messiah

Echoes of Thunder

1. "Suppose Jesus came to your church. I don't mean symbolically. I mean visibly. Physically. Actually."
   A. Try to imagine the above scene. What would Jesus look like? What would he do?
   B. How do you think your church would react? Why?

2. "It's easy to criticize contemporaries of Jesus for not believing in him. But when you realize how he came, you can understand their skepticism."
   A. What is it about Jesus' coming that would make skepticism understandable, if not excusable?
   B. Try to put yourself back in first-century Israel. How do you think you would have seen Jesus? Explain.

3. "We still think we know which phone God uses and which car he drives. We still think we know what he looks like. But he's been known to surprise us."
   A. What does Max mean in his first two sentences above?

B. How has God been known to surprise you?

4. "When we let God define himself, a whole new world opens before us."
   A. How do we let God define himself?
   B. Why does a new world open before us when we let God define himself?

5. "The old man saw Jesus because he didn't know what he looked like. The people in Jesus' day missed him because they thought they did."
   A. How can we find God if we don't know what his appearances will look like?
   B. What lessons can we learn from Max's insight above?

Flashes of Lightning

1. Read John 7:25–29.
   A. What did the people start to suspect in verse 25? Why did they change their minds in verse 27?
   B. How does Jesus use their questions to make a claim about himself? What claim does he make?

2. Read Luke 7:33–35.
   A. What was the people's objection to John the Baptist (verse 33)?
   B. What was the people's objection to Jesus (verse 34)?
   C. What conclusion does Jesus make (verse 35)?

3. Read Matthew 25:34–45.
   A. How does this passage teach us it is possible to be in contact with Jesus today and yet not recognize him?
   B. How can this result in both good and bad consequences?

Chapter 27   Peter, Me, and Wile E. Coyote

Echoes of Thunder

1. "Like Wile E. we fall. But unlike Wile E., we wander in the canyon for a while. Stunned, hurt . . . and wondering if this ravine has a way out."
   A. What kind of "canyons" have you wandered in? What pulled you out?
   B. In what ways are you and Wile E. Coyote alike? In what ways are you different?

2. "When we fall, we can dismiss it. We can deny it. We can distort it. Or we can deal with it."
   A. How do we dismiss our falls? How do we deny them? How do we distort them?
   B. What is the best way to deal with our falls? Is this easy? Explain.

3. "We keep no secrets from God. Confession is not telling God what we did. He already knows. Confession is simply agreeing with God that our acts were wrong."
   A. Do you think this is a good definition of confession? Explain.
   B. Why does God insist that we confess our sins?

4. "Mingle the tears of the sinner with the cross of the Savior and the result is a joyful escort out of the canyon of guilt."
   A. How do the tears of a sinner and the cross of the Savior combine to bring joy?
   B. Have you known this joy that Max talks about? Explain.

Flashes of Lightning

1. Read John 18:25–27.
   A. What kind of stumbling is described here?
   B. Could it have been prevented? If so, how?

2. Read Luke 22:61.
   A. What kind of look do you think the Lord gave to Peter? Explain.
   B. What effect did this look have on Peter? Why do you think it had this effect?

3. Read 2 Corinthians 7:8–11.
   A. What did Paul do as described in verse 8? How did he feel about this?
   B. What was the result of Paul's action? How did this make him feel?
   C. What principle is laid out in verse 10?
   D. How is this principle "fleshed out" in verse 11?

Chapter 28   Ready for Home

Echoes of Thunder

1. "We sometimes act as if the Christian life is a retirement cruise."

A. What does Max mean by his statement above?

B. Have you ever seen Christians acting out this statement? Have you ever been tempted to do so? Explain.

2. "When the freeze comes, we step out on the ice with forks, games, and skimpy clothing, and pass our final days walking against the wind, often blaming God for getting us into this mess."

A. What times of "freezing" have you experienced in your own life?

B. Why does it seem so easy for us to blame God for things that are not his doing?

3. "Why was the salvation of his soul so urgent after the shot and so optional before it? Why had he postponed his decision to accept Christ until his deathbed? Because he assumed he had time."

A. How often do you think we make the same mistake the general did? Why do we make this mistake?

B. What are some effective ways to demonstrate the danger of this kind of mistake? If you were working with someone who also assumed he had time, what would you do?

4. "What supplies are you taking? Are you carrying your share of silver and games? Don't be fooled; they may matter here, but they matter not when you reach your Father's house. What matters is if you are known by the Father."

A. What supplies are you taking?

B. Are you known by the Father? How do you know for sure?

Flashes of Lightning

1. Read Psalm 27:7–14.
   A. What requests does the psalmist make in verses 7–9 and 11–12?
   B. What expectation does he have in verse 10?
   C. What hope does he have in verse 13?
   D. What advice does he give in verse 14?

2. Read James 1:13–16.
   A. What are some of us prone to do when we get into trouble (verse 13)?
   B. How does James respond to this?
   C. What warning does he give in verse 16? Why put this here?

3. Read James 4:13–16.
   A. Why is it foolish to plan ahead without taking God into consideration?
   B. What instead should be our attitude?

Chapter 29   The Cave People

Echoes of Thunder

1. "The sounds in the cave were mournful, but the people didn't know it, for they had never known joy. The spirit in the cave was death, but the people didn't know it, for they had never known life."
   A. How can someone not know their true condition?
   B. What people do you know who are unaware of their true condition?

2. "Light always hurts before it helps," he answered. "Step closer. The pain will soon pass."
   A. Why does "light" always hurt before it helps? What does the light represent in this parable?
   B. How does light finally help? How important is the pain? Explain.

3. "Carry this to your people. Tell them the light is here and the light is warm. Tell them the light is for all who desire it."
   A. What is the point of this passage?
   B. What light have you been asked to carry to your own people? Who are your own people? Are they seeing light in your hands? Explain.

Flashes of Lightning

1. Read John 1:3–13.
   A. In what way is Jesus our light?
   B. How are men prone to respond to this light (verses 10–11)?
   C. What promise is given in verses 12–13?

2. Read Romans 1:13–17.
   A. What was Paul's goal in verse 13?
   B. What was Paul's attitude in verses 14–15?
   C. What was Paul's confidence in verses 16–17?

3. Read 1 Corinthians 9:19–23.

A. What was Paul's commitment in verse 19?
B. What was Paul's method in verses 20–22?
C. What was Paul's goal in verse 23?

Chapter 30   If Only You Knew

Echoes of Thunder

1. "I was being kind. The bird thought I was cruel."
    A. What was the bird probably thinking?
    B. How are we often like the bird when God is trying to deal with us?

2. "If only we could learn to trust him. But how hard it is."
    A. Why is trusting God hard for many of us?
    B. How can we learn to trust God more?

3. "His thunder is still gentle. And his gentleness still thunders."
    A. In what way is God's "thunder" gentle?
    B. In what way does God's gentleness "thunder"?

4. "The gift and the Giver. If you know them, you know all you need."
    A. What is the gift Max mentions? Who is the Giver? What is crucial about both of them?
    B. Do you know this gift and this Giver? How do you know for sure?

Flashes of Lightning

1. Read John 4:10–15, 23–26.
    A. What kind of water did the woman want? What kind of water did Jesus offer her?
    B. What is the Father seeking, according to verse 23?
    C. What claim did Jesus make for himself in verse 26?

2. Read Jeremiah 29:11.
    A. What kind of plans does the Lord have for us?
    B. How does this make you feel? Why?

3. Read Psalm 9:10.
    A. Who will trust the Lord? What does this mean?
    B. Whom does the Lord never forsake? Does this include you? Why or why not?

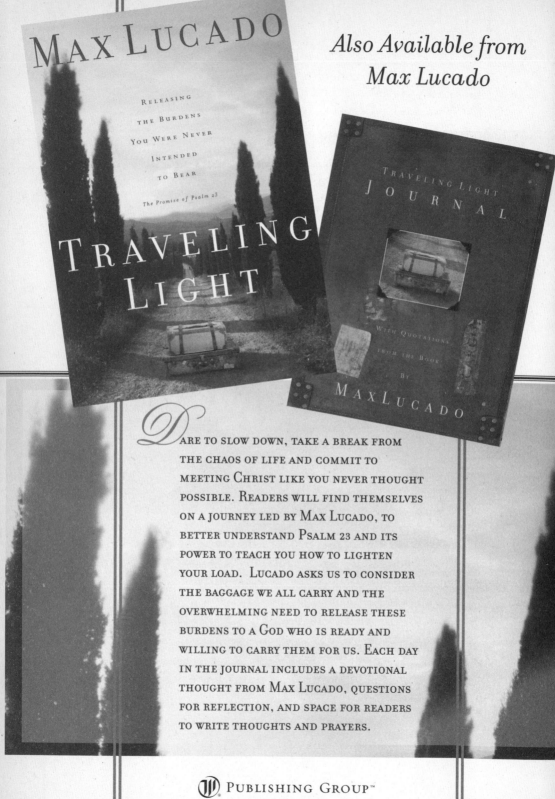

MAX LUCADO

RELEASING
THE BURDENS
YOU WERE NEVER
INTENDED
TO BEAR

The Promise of Psalm 23

TRAVELING
LIGHT

*Also Available from
Max Lucado*

TRAVELING LIGHT
JOURNAL

WITH QUOTATIONS
FROM THE BOOK
BY
MAX LUCADO

ARE TO SLOW DOWN, TAKE A BREAK FROM
THE CHAOS OF LIFE AND COMMIT TO
MEETING CHRIST LIKE YOU NEVER THOUGHT
POSSIBLE. READERS WILL FIND THEMSELVES
ON A JOURNEY LED BY MAX LUCADO, TO
BETTER UNDERSTAND PSALM 23 AND ITS
POWER TO TEACH YOU HOW TO LIGHTEN
YOUR LOAD. LUCADO ASKS US TO CONSIDER
THE BAGGAGE WE ALL CARRY AND THE
OVERWHELMING NEED TO RELEASE THESE
BURDENS TO A GOD WHO IS READY AND
WILLING TO CARRY THEM FOR US. EACH DAY
IN THE JOURNAL INCLUDES A DEVOTIONAL
THOUGHT FROM MAX LUCADO, QUESTIONS
FOR REFLECTION, AND SPACE FOR READERS
TO WRITE THOUGHTS AND PRAYERS.

 PUBLISHING GROUP™
www.wpublishinggroup.com